Old New England Homes

by

Stanley Schuler

Schiffer Publishing Ltd

Box E. Exton, Pennsylvania 19341

Other books by Stanley Schuler published by Schiffer

American Barns
The Cape Cod House
Coal Heat
Mississippi Valley Architecture

Printed in the United States of America.
ISBN: 0-88740-034-5
Published by Schiffer Publishing Ltd. 1469 Morstein Road, West Chester, Pennsylvania 19380

This book may be purchased from the publisher.
Please include $1.50 postage.
Try your bookstore first.

TABLE OF CONTENTS

NEW ENGLAND ARCHITECTURE
1620-1900

Put yourself in the Pilgrims' shoes. It's late December. You've just reached a new world, strange and frightening. You've had a long, hard, anxious voyage.

The first thing you're going to do is to thank God you've arrived safely. (Actually, the Pilgrims did this when they first anchored off Cape Cod. But they undoubtedly did it again when they reached Plymouth harbor.)

The next thing you do is to study the country that is going to be your home. The hills, the great trees, the rocks, the stream tumbling out of the hills.

Then, after you've settled where you're going to establish your village, you take whatever steps you can quickly to protect yourself against the unknown, fearsome people that inhabit North America.

Then you think about getting some decent food into your belly.

And only then are you going to worry about shelter. But you're not going to be very fussy about what kind of shelter so long as it keeps off rain and snow and allows you to stay reasonably warm. (On the Mayflower you've been exposed for so long to rain, wind and cold and water splashing over the ship and into the hold that a little more of the same doesn't bother you very much.)

Here is the basic explanation for why we today do not find houses dating from the first days that America was settled. Shelter was important to the Pilgrims (and to the people that followed after them and those that preceded them to Jamestown) but it had a fairly low priority. There was too much else for the Pilgrims to think and worry about first. They could and would and did make do in huts and hovels until more important things were well in hand.

The oldest known New England house that is still standing was built in 1636. It is the Fairbanks house in Dedham, Massachusetts. After 1636, the construction of substantial houses increased but to what extent we can only guess. Fire, storm, decay, demolition have taken most of them. I can count only about two hundred existing New England houses that were built before 1700. There may be more but not many.

However, those that are left are an interesting lesson in the development of New England architecture.

The earliest houses were a direct throwback to the English houses of the same and previous eras. Of Jacobean, or medieval, design, they were the only houses that the first settlers were familiar with and knew how to build. It must have occurred to some of them that since they were now living in a new world it would be a nice idea to own a new kind of house. But they probably didn't know what it should be and in the circumstances they probably didn't think change was important. On the contrary, they had already made such an enormous and at times terrifying change just in moving to a new world that they were quite content with the kind of house they well understood.

Warm, dry, comfortable shelter was all they really wanted. So the houses they put up were almost identical with those they had left behind. These were small but had one-and-a-half or two stories surmounted by a steep roof with a rather massive chimney. They were only one room deep. Most started with a single room on each floor (so-called half houses) but some had two. In the former, the fireplace and chimney were in one of the end walls. In the latter, on the first floor, the "hall", which did double-duty as the kitchen, was at one side of the central chimney and the parlor, which served also as a bedroom, was at the other. Upstairs were two bedrooms reached by a very steep stair rising usually from a tiny entrance hall in front of the chimney. Since the builders were much more concerned with function than appearance, the front door was often off-center in the facade and the windows were likely to be placed willy-nilly. There was little symmetry.

Although in English houses of the 1600s the roofline was often broken by large gables, the American colonists generally settled for a more easily constructed unbroken, straight roofline. But they frequently did follow the English practice of projecting the second floor a foot or more beyond the first. In some cases this overhang, or jetty, was used only at the front; in others, it was also at one or both ends.

Windows were few and very small, the better to protect against Indian attack and keep out cold. When the home owners could finally afford it, they filled the openings with leaded casements. Before that they simply used shutters and/or oiled paper.

Construction was with wood as it was in England until the middle of the Seventeenth Century and, of course, because wood was so plentiful in America. Houses were framed with huge oak timbers carefully fitted together. Between the uprights the walls were filled with wattle and daub (twigs and clay) or sundried bricks of varying sizes and shapes. To protect this inner lining against moisture and as greater protection against cold, walls were clad on the exterior with short hand-hewn clapboards (in this respect the houses were unlike their English predecessors) and on the interior with wide boards. Roofs were initially thatched, but this material was soon replaced by wood shingles.

When a two-room house became too small for its owner, the logical way to enlarge it was, first, to add a second set of rooms that more or less matched the first at the back of the fireplace, thus lengthening the house. Then, when another addition was called for, the owner, following English practice, built a leanto on the back of the house, either at one end or across the entire back. This was easily done by carrying the rear slope of the main roof down toward the ground to create a "catslide". Thus was born the saltbox. It proved to be such a good way to build a large house that it wasn't long before many New England houses were built as saltboxes to start with.

Here is one example of how the New England Colonial house evolved. In this case, the evolutionary process seems completely logical and understandable. But how do we explain the development of other types of Colonial house — the simple two-story house, the story-and-a-half Cape Cod house and the garrison house?

Actually, the garrison house presents no mysteries. It did not evolve; it just sprang into existence to meet a special need. The date was about 1650; the location, the thinly settled backwoods. The Indians, having become fed up with the settlers, had at last developed murderous designs toward them. The settlers' answer was to enclose the settlement in a stockade within which was a garrison house that everyone could retire to when attack was threatened.

The garrison house did not differ greatly

from others of the period, yet it did not look like a Jacobean house. It was one-and-a-half or two stories tall. If two stories, the upper overhung the lower, but apparently not for reasons of defense; it just happened that the period in which garrison houses were built was also the period in which overhangs were most popular. The roof was a little less steep than in the Jacobean house and was probably never thatched because thatch could too easily be set afire by the Indians. However, since wood shingles were also combustible, the settlers constructed the attic floor of heavy timbers that were kept covered with sand or ashes to protect the space below. But the most notable characteristic of the garrison house was the exterior walls. These were formidable — made of square-hewn horizontal logs fitted tight together but pierced here and there by holes just large enough to sight a musket through. The few windows were tiny.

Today, in the very few garrison houses that remain, the logs are usually sheathed with boards. As a result, the houses have no obvious distinguishing characteristics.

The two-story Colonial and Cape Cod houses are quite another matter. Both are distinctive. Both evolved gradually. Just how gradually is indicated by the fact that houses of Jacobean design were built long after the first Colonial houses appeared. This is hardly surprising. Even today styles do not change completely overnight; and in Seventeenth Century America abrupt change was impossible for a number of reasons: The settlers were soon widely scattered and new ideas traveled at snail's pace between them. Since they were an unpretentious, conservative, cautious folk, they did not accept new ideas readily. Finally, because newcomers with old ideas were flooding in from England, old ideas about building were long in the ascendancy.

Even so, the inevitable change in house design was slowly taking place because experience in America showed that Jacobean design was no longer suitable. Consider, for example, the second-story overhang. No one today is quite sure why European houses were built with this. It may have been because lots in European towns were cramped; therefore second stories had to be enlarged to create more total living space. It may have been because houses were taxed on the amount of land they covered and this was one way to get more house at lower taxes. It may have been to protect the first floor, which was not covered with siding, from weather. It may have been because the long timbers used for corner posts had become scarce: jettying made it possible to use the available short timbers and gain needed interior space without weakening the structure. Or it may have been simply to make houses more interesting in appearance, prettier. In any case, none of these reasons for an overhang was important in vast, heavily timbered America. Therefore, the overhang disappeared.

Similarly, the extremely steep roof of the Jacobean house disappeared because thatching lost favor in New England about forty years after the Pilgrims landed. Because of its inherent porosity, a thatched roof had to be steep to shed water rapidly. But when the colonists switched to wood — a far better roofing material — roof pitch could be lowered.

Similarly, windows grew larger and more numerous as fears of Indian attack abated. Furthermore, because of the cold New England climate, increased fenestration particularly on the south sides of houses (New Englanders always tried to face their houses south) was needed to bring in more of the sun's heat in winter.

Finally, the colonists undoubtedly desired greater simplicity in the design of their homes. This may be partly attributed to their Puritanical beliefs: they were austere, no-nonsense people under the discipline of a harsh church and they strove for modesty in everything from personal character to clothing to houses. But the trend to a simpler house design must also have been dictated by the busy life everyone led. There just wasn't time or money to indulge in the relatively complicated construction of a Jacobean house when an equally good or better house could be built by simplifying the design.

For all these reasons the style of New England houses changed from Jacobean to Colonial. The approximate date was 1700.

Most architectural histories give the impression that there was only one style of New England Colonial house — the two-story structure, which would also include the saltbox since it was merely a variant of the familiar two-story Colonial. Actually, there was another style that is now known across the country as the Cape, or more properly, as the Cape Cod house. Why architectural historians generally ignore it I do not know — perhaps because it is also considered a variant of the two-story house. But whereas the saltbox differed from the standard two-story Colonial only in that it had an elongated catslide roof in the rear (looking at the house head on you can't tell it isn't a standard Colonial), the Cape Cod house differed in that it was only a story-and-a-half high and came in three common sizes. For this reason, the two-story Colonial and the Cape should be considered as two distinct types of one basic style.

Both are Colonial — that must be emphasized. In general plan and many details they are alike. But they are at the same time different.

All American Colonial styles were severe; the New England style most of all. These were very simple, austere, symmetrical, rectangular houses. They had no ornamentation; what little trim they had was made of smooth, flat boards.

In the typical two-story house, the door, often with a fixed transom of small glass panes, was centered in the facade and flanked on either side by two double-hung windows in which only the bottom sash slid; the upper was fixed. The windows were glazed with 6 x 8-inch rectangular panes. In the earliest houses there were usually nine panes in the upper sash and six in the lower, or vice versa. Later, the arrangement was twelve over eight or eight over twelve. But all Colonial windows were distinguished by the fact that the mullions were quite thick, with the glass set close to the outer edges. And in a great many houses the windows projected about two inches out from the walls and had no surrounding casings. This was because the walls were only about three inches thick.

Windows on the second floor were placed directly under the eaves, which projected only a few inches beyond the walls.

The roof, in nine cases out of ten, was a simple steep gable; in the other cases it was a gambrel. Dormers were rare. But the brick or sometimes stone chimney was always large — often massive — and was almost always centered between the ends of the ridge (therefore directly in line with the door).

The plan of the houses was about as simple and unvaried as the exterior. Entering the door, you stepped into a tiny hall from which a very steep stairway rose to the upper floor. To one side of the entry was the parlor; to the other, the "hall". Both had fireplaces built into the enormous chimney block. Across the back of the house was a long kitchen with a buttery (pantry) and/or tiny bedroom (now usually called the borning room) at one end; or sometimes the buttery was at one end and the bedroom at the other. The kitchen also had a fireplace big enough to be used for cooking vented into the central chimney. The upstairs was divided into several chambers, of which at least one usually had a fireplace.

Like its English forebears, the house was constructed of great oak timbers neatly joined and pegged together. Rising from the sills were the four two-story-high corner posts and — in the front and back walls — a pair of intermediate posts set in line with the sides of the chimney. All the posts were joined together at the second-story level by girts and at the top by a matching system of plates. Thus was formed the framework of a large box. The intermediate posts were joined, front to back, by chimney girts. Summer beams, the largest of all the timbers, were laid from the midpoint of the chimney girts to the midpoint of the nearest end girts. (In a few houses, however, the summer beams ran across the house rather than lengthwise.) The joists were laid at right angles to the summer beams and notched into them and the front and rear girts and plates to form a level base for the second and attic floors. (On the ground floor the summer beams were eliminated and the joists were parallel with the front and back walls of the house.)

The roof was laid on oak rafters roughly twice the size of those used today. There were four or more, and while in better houses they were usually hewn into rectangles, in others they were simply left round and flattened on the upper side. Instead of being joined to a ridge board, the opposite pairs were fastened directly together. If the rafters were spaced only three or four feet apart, the roof was completed by laying sheathing boards across them and then applying shingles. On the other hand, when there were only a few rafters widely spaced, horizontal purlins were notched into them and the sheathing was done with thick boards laid vertically.

Exterior walls were clad in somewhat similar fashion. If studs were installed between the posts, clapboards were nailed directly to them. Wall sheathing did not come into widespread use until after the Revolution. In plank-frame houses on the other hand, there were no studs at all. Their place was taken by 1½ to 2-inch-thick vertical planks extending from the sills to the plates. Clapboards were nailed to these.

Clapboards were for a long time the favored siding material. Although some early houses were shingled, widespread use of shingles was a later development. At first the clapboards were made of riven oak; then pine and cedar came into use. Just why the clapboards on some houses were graduated — that is, the exposure of those at the base of the wall was only about two inches while the exposure at eight-foot level was 2½ inches and that at the top of the wall was almost four inches — is unclear. The greater thickness of wood certainly helped to keep the first floor warmer, but if this was the home owner's primary aim, he would have graduated the clapboards on all four walls. Actually, he restricted the practice to the front of the house; consequently it must be considered mainly decorative.

The Cape Cod house was merely a smaller version of the two-story house. Many historians say it was built close to the ground and only one-and-a-half stories high so that it could better withstand Cape Cod's howling winds and storms. But this ignores an important point: The Cape Cod name to the contrary, no one has proved that the house originated on the Cape. It just happens to have been built there in greater numbers than elsewhere in New England. As I found when writing my previous book, *The Cape Cod House*, the earliest Cape Cod houses still standing were built in 1666 in Old Lyme, Connecticut — twelve years before the Saconesset Homestead at West Falmouth, the oldest extant Cape on Cape Cod. Furthermore, there are numerous other very early Capes elsewhere in Massachusetts as well as in Connecticut and Maine. Many of these are miles back from the ocean and its strong winds.

The inevitable conclusion is that these

little houses were not dictated primarily by the weather. Instead they were built to save money.

Aside from its reduced stature (the front and rear walls were only about 8 feet high, and the roof peak was only about 20 feet above ground level), the Cape Cod house had several unique characteristics.

It literally hugged the ground. This was especially true of the houses on Cape Cod, where early builders often omitted foundations and built on oak sills resting on piles of rocks dug into the ground. (In some instances they may have laid the sills right on the ground.)

The gable roofs were often — but not invariably — bowed. In some houses such as the Jabez Wilder house, this upward curve of each roof slope is pronounced. In most cases, however, it is so slight as to be almost unnoticeable. In no case is there an obvious explanation. Popular theory has it that the shipwrights that built many of the houses just shaped the roofs as they did hulls. That is a possibility. Or were the roofs bowed because some early English roofs were bowed? Or was the bow designed to increase attic headroom? Or was it meant simply to give the roof greater strength by increasing its resistance to compression? We don't know.

The windows in the gables were placed in pleasantly eccentric fashion. In the typical arrangement there were two big windows in the middle, a small window on either side and a fifth very small window centered under the roof peak. But other arrangements, even including tiny triangular windows, were also used.

In the standard Cape, also known as the full Cape, the front door was centered in the facade and flanked by a pair of windows on either side. The great chimney was centered on the ridge above the door. This was the largest Cape. It measured approximately 34 to 40 feet long and 28 feet deep — about the same dimensions as a two-story Colonial with a conventional gable roof (saltboxes, naturally, were much deeper).

But Capes were also built in three smaller sizes.

In the three-quarter Cape — about 28 feet long — the off-center door was flanked on one side by a single window and on the other by a pair. The chimney was centered above the door. Except for the fact that the front room at the short side of the door and the kitchen area were reduced in size, the plan of the three-quarter Cape was like that of the full Cape.

In the half Cape, however, the door was at one end of the house and there were only two front windows grouped together on the other side. The chimney was usually at the same end of the house as the door but might be at the opposite end. The whole house was about 20 feet long and there was only one front room with a small kitchen plus, perhaps, a bedroom and buttery behind it.

Still smaller was the quarter Cape, which was laid out like a half Cape but had just one window in the facade. It is quite rare, although it probably was more prevalent in early days. Also rare today as well as in the past was the double Cape, consisting of two full Capes joined end to end.

Excepting those that were burned or torn down, the main reason why we today find few quarter Capes and not a great many half Capes is that they were subsequently enlarged. This was done by extending the house beyond the chimney end. However, most Capes, like most two-story Colonials, were expanded by adding an ell to the back of the house, usually at one corner so it would not block off the kitchen windows. To this ell, as time went on, other additions were made; with the result that the houses often became much deeper than they were long.

Still, there is no mistaking a Cape Cod house. Despite its simplicity it is a lovely little building that was popular for about 130 years. Then, after a hundred-year hiatus, it was revived during the Great Depression and was put up in greater numbers than ever. No style of house has been more widely built in the United States.

Its only close rivals have been the two-story Colonials and two-story Georgians, which probably are still more widely built in New England than even the so-called ranch house of the post-World War II era.

The Georgian style of architecture coincided with the Colonial. In America it began in 1700 in Virginia and drew to a close shortly after the Revolution.

In contrast with Colonial houses, Georgian houses were high fashion — richly, although often sparingly, ornamented. The style, derived largely from Andrea Palladio's interpretations of Roman forms, originated with Sir Christopher Wren and his followers and was brought to America in innumerable books from which American builders copied. Although the style is associated mainly with the country's great houses — the mansions of the wealthy — there were many small and medium-size New England homes that were also Georgian. Most of these appear at hasty glance to be standard two-story Colonials but on longer look turn out to be Georgian because they have a handsome, sometimes elaborate doorway and/or they have two chimneys placed more or less at the ends of the roof. And if you go inside, you may find other Georgian touches even though the houses may still be Colonial in plan.

In other words, it is not always easy to differentiate between Colonial houses and modest Georgian houses. The Georgian mansions, however, are another matter.

Since they were deeper than Colonial homes, they were more nearly square. They had four rooms of roughly equal size on each floor. These were arranged two on each side of a central stair hall that ran from the front to the back of the house. Because of the halls, circulation and privacy in the houses were improved: it was no longer necessary to walk through one room to reach another.

While most Georgian houses in the South were built of brick, those in the North were wood-clad. A few of these look as if they have masonry walls; but they are actually sided with wide, flat boards with deep V joints on the sides, at the ends and up and down between the ends, thus giving the effect of large stone blocks laid in a common masonry bond. (This is called rusticated siding.) Most houses, however, were covered with narrow clapboards.

In keeping with the floor plan, Georgian facades were symmetrical. The central doorway was flanked by double-hung windows that were a little bigger than Colonial windows and had larger panes. Upper-story windows were neatly aligned with those below.

Gambrel and hip roofs were the rule. Hip roofs were often crowned by a balustrade that formed a widow's, or captain's, walk; and sometimes, for ornament, a balustrade encircled the roof above the eaves. Dormer windows were common. Central chimneys were less so. There were at least two chimneys and occasionally four. These were placed either at the very ends of the house flush with the walls or within several feet of the walls.

The roofs did not terminate simply and abruptly at the eaves. Georgian houses are noted for their handsome classical cornices adorned with a continuous string of large blocks known as modillions. Dentils, other moldings and even carvings might also be employed.

Doorways were always given great prominence. They might be topped by gorgeous pediments and edged by pilasters or engaged columns (in effect, columns split down the middle and attached to the walls like pilasters). Or they might be protected by a columned portico. Or together with the nearest windows, they might be centered in a pavilion that projected slightly from the facade and was capped at roof height by a large pediment.

Windows were framed by architraves (ornamental moldings) and often headed by small pediments or cornices. When dormers were used, their roofs frequently were alternately pitched and barrel-shaped. And many houses boasted a Palladian window consisting of a central high, arched window sandwiched between smaller, narrow, rectangular windows.

Finally, the walls of the great houses were often relieved by enormous pilasters. These were generally placed at the front corners and sometimes were used on either side of a pavilion. If corner pilasters were not used, their places might be taken by quoins.

Interiors were no less decorative. In fact, many of the most beautiful rooms in the United States are found in Georgian homes.

Until about the middle of the Eighteenth Century, walls were usually paneled. This, of course, was not the simple vertical board paneling popular today. Here magnificent wood panels with chamfered edges were set in wide frames of matching wood. This sort of paneling was used in virtually all Georgian houses, but in the second half of the century it began to give way to plastered walls covered with wallpaper imported from abroad or, in some cases, made in America.

Handsome cornices encircled ceilings and in some of the mansions the ceilings themselves were covered by intricate *rocaille* work consisting of garlands, leaves, geometric figures, etc., superimposed on the plaster.

Fireplaces were a far cry from the simple brick or stone, oak-linteled fireplaces in Colonial homes. Few Georgian fireplaces attained the enormous size of the Colonial kitchen fireplace, but because of their mantels they gave the appearance of being bigger than they were. In other words, after the Georgian style was in full swing, the mantels were large and ornate. These were surmounted by equally ornate mantelshelves. And above the shelves, affixed to the chimney breast, were chimneypieces that rivaled any of the paintings we customarily use in their place today.

The stairways in the great houses were equally wondrous. Since they were straight and made right-angle turns, they were not so graceful as curving stairs. Instead they imparted a sense of great strength and practicality. What made them beautiful were the banisters and particularly the balusters, which were commonly placed three to a step. Because of their cost we shall probably never see their like again. In some cases they were turned, as today, at right angles to the grain of the wood. But frequently, thanks to the influence of an English book popular with American artisans, they were turned in spirals. In a number of houses three different spiral patterns were grouped on each tread.

Newel posts in many instances were similarly treated. And as if this were not enough decoration, fancy scrolls were applied to the stringers below each stair tread.

Although simple Colonial houses outnumbered Georgian houses because the John Does of early America outnumbered the wealthy merchants and planters, Georgian was the dominant architectural style in America just because it was the one espoused by America's leaders — the trend-setters. But Georgian was an English style, often rather heavy handed despite its beauty. And at the end of the Revolutionary War, the newly freed colonists were fed up with the heavy-handed British. They were establishing a new nation, setting out on a new way of life, and they were looking for a new style of architecture. They found it for several decades in the Federal.

Ironically, the Federal style was largely English, too. Its originators were James and Robert (mainly Robert) Adam, a pair of Scots. But it was turned into an American style by Charles Bulfinch, Samuel McIntire, Asher Benjamin and others. Although it became a nationwide style, it was, because of these New England architects, at its best in New England.

The hallmarks of the Federal style were freedom and delicacy. The new freedom was most evident in the floor plans. The typical Federal house was more or less square, with two rooms on either side of a central stair hall. But in many of the houses built by the wealthy, one or more of the main rooms — usually the *salon* — was elliptical, oval or circular and projected from the flat walls toward the street or garden. A few of these rooms even had high domed ceilings.

Many stair halls were also of elliptical or oval design. Or to improve privacy and circulation, stairs were removed entirely from the entrance hall and relegated to a separate space. A second stairway was added so that the servants and their activities were not always on public view. Also in the interest of minimizing the sight and sound of servants, a pantry was placed between the kitchen and dining room. And to discourage casual visitors from entering directly into family life, the main living area was in some houses moved to the second floor.

Family convenience and privacy were also improved by designing rooms for a single purpose. Instead of having the main rooms face the street, they were often moved to the garden side — particularly if this was the south side. Bedrooms were arranged in suites, sometimes with dressing rooms. Alcoves were made for beds and the dining room sideboard.

In short, the planning of houses was given the same sort of thought we give it today. This was in sharp contrast to the past.

The change in the exterior appearance of Federal houses was less sharp — especially in the case of smaller houses, which often look like slightly-dressed-up versions of Colonial homes. Nevertheless, study of Federal houses shows a distinct change.

Roofs were low-pitched and frequently hipped. On the largest houses, which were three and occasionally four stories high, the roofs were almost invisible from the street because they were so low and also because they were sometimes encircled by a balustrade. This latter feature was, of course, not new; but whereas in Georgian houses it had been composed of identical balusters neatly spaced from roof end to roof end, after 1800 it was a popular practice to break up the balustrade with large, usually solid panels.

The elaborate Georgian cornices below the roof were simplified and made somewhat smaller and more delicate. The chimneys at the ends of the house were tall and slender.

Although a few more houses were built of brick than in the past, the majority were clapboarded. (The use of flat bevel-edged boards to resemble large cut stones came to an end.) Ornamentation was generally limited to splayed lintels over the windows. When columns were used — usually to support the rectangular or semi-circular roofs of the small porticos protecting the front doors (a very common feature of houses built after 1780) —they were slender and finely detailed. Most were of Ionic or Corinthian design.

The Palladian window virtually disappeared, but other windows had an airier, more graceful look than their predecessors. Panes were larger; muntins, thinner. Ground floor windows were often centered in or under large, slightly recessed arches. If the main living area was on the second floor, the front windows on that floor were lengthened so the owners could step out onto balconies. In the three-story houses, window heights at the different levels varied, with the top story having the shortest windows. Square-headed triple windows were used to increase light and air in the house.

The principal decorative feature of all Federal houses was the doorway. This was more delicately designed than the handsome Georgian doorways, and even the simplest has an elegance that turns your head when you pass. In the great houses, which were commonly raised well above ground, the entrances were approached by a graceful flight of steps or even more graceful pair of steps leading to the entrance platform. The single or double door was flanked by slender sidelights and almost invariably by a fanlight. Early in the Federal period the fanlights were fully semi-circular but they became elliptical or segmental (reduced to part of a semi-circle) after the turn of the Nineteenth Century. The glass was set in lovely lead tracery.

The delicacy of the doorways was repeated inside the house.

Because stair halls were no longer rectangular, the stairs themselves lost their angularity. They swept upward in a lovely curve. Or they might run straight for a short distance, curve into another straight run, curve again, and so on to the top. In keeping with this new design, the balusters were slimmed down and simplified. And because the wall below the inner side of the stairway was often omitted, the entire stairway seemed to float.

Fireplace design was similarly simplified. Since the chimneypiece of the Georgian period was eliminated, eyes dwell on the mantelpiece alone. This is a most satisfying sight. The heavy Georgian look is gone. All the traditional elements of the mantelpiece are still there — the flanking upright supports consisting of pilasters, panels or slender colonettes; the wide frieze across the top of the fireplace opening; and the mantelshelf — but the way in which they were tied together was exemplary. Even without ornamentation

the mantelpiece was charming. But the carved garlands, swags, festoons, medallions and figures applied to the uprights and primarily to the frieze made it a work of art. How much of this ornamentation was used depended on the architect and wealth of the home owner but it was never overdone. There was no overcrowding.

Indeed, the lack of overcrowding is a characteristic of New England Federal rooms. Ceilings, for instance, might be ornamented with plaster appliques but these were placed in the center of the ceiling and perhaps near the corners so that they stood out against the smooth plaster. Walls, too, were mainly smooth plaster (often papered) and topped by chaste cornices.

The Federal style was quiet elegance.

The Greek Revival style that followed in 1820 and ran to about 1860 was elegant also but in a monumental way.

While the Georgian and Federal styles were interpretations of classical forms, Greek Revival was a direct throwback to ancient Greece, Rome and, in rare instances, Egypt. (Because three ancient nations, not just Greece, contributed to the style, some people prefer to call Greek Revival a Classic Revival style; and some even break the style down into three styles — Greek, Roman and Egyptian. But the favored name is Greek Revival.)

Greek Revival owes its genesis to Washington and Jefferson, both of whom felt that a new nation should have a new architecture — something expressing the monumentality, simplicity, purity and dignity of the ancient world. Since Jefferson himself was an architect, the style first took hold in the South, from where it spread gradually across the entire country. But New England home owners received it with somewhat less enthusiasm than those in other sections. This was probably attributable to the people's conservatism and great — and still abiding

— love of Colonial, Georgian and Federal.

This is not to say that Greek Revival architecture is rare in the region. It was very popular for churches and all other types of public building. And while Greek Revival houses are scarce in Boston, they are relatively common in towns founded long after Boston and in seacoast communities, where men were made wealthy by whaling just at the time the style was taking hold throughout the country.

Be this as it may, when you come upon a pure Greek Revival house in New England you cannot mistake it. (Other houses of earlier design were given a Greek Revival look by additions and alterations.) It's not always big but it is bold, broad, severe and handsome — suggestive of a temple.

Its most notable feature is large columns or pilasters set beneath a classic entablature. All the orders were used — Doric, Ionic, Corinthian, Tuscan and Composite — but these were normally Americanized. Usually made of wood, the columns in the great houses rose a full two stories in even spacing across the front of a fairly shallow porch. Pilasters might be equally large and were also evenly spaced across the facade, thus dividing it clearly into bays. (The typical house, as in earlier times, had five bays. The middle bay incorporated the door; each of the others had a window.) On one-story houses, of course, the columns and pilasters were scaled down.

The houses were rectangular and, as a rule, were set with the short side facing the street. Thus the ridge of the roof, which was usually pitched but might be hipped, was perpendicular to the street. This meant, in turn, that in houses with pitched roofs the entablature was surmounted by a pedimented gable. In hip-roof houses, on the other hand, there was a low parapet above the entablature. Cornices in all cases were heavy and masculine.

Whatever the roof form, it has less pitch than in preceding architectural styles and might be almost totally invisible from the ground either from the two sides in the case of gable roofs or from all four sides in the case of hip roofs. Nevertheless, this did not necessarily eliminate attics or even sleeping rooms under the roof. In some cases these were made habitable by large central cupolas, or lanterns. In other cases, light and air were admitted through rows of small lie-on-the-stomach windows that pierced the friezes below the eaves.

Ideally, exterior walls were as smooth and untextured as possible, but the ideal was attained only when they were covered with flush board siding. A fair number of houses were treated in this way, but others were built of brick or square-cut stone and many were clapboarded. Even against such rougher materials, the doorways and windows stood out boldly. Since the ancient Greeks did not use arches, there were no arched doors, windows or other features in Greek Revival architecture. The square-headed windows, which were about the same size as Federal windows, were topped by emphatic stone lintels in masonry houses or by heavy pediments in wood houses. Similarly, doorways formed an uncompromising rectangle of considerable size, because the doors were flanked by sidelights and headed by an elongated transom light.

In plan, New England's Greek Revival homes were little different from Federal homes. The modest house typically had four rooms and a central hall. In larger houses, the plan was more irregular; all rooms served a specific purpose; and some were round or oval. A good many two-story houses were built with or soon acquired one-story side wings. Some were L or T shaped. And in northern New England, the occasional Greek Revival farmhouse was likely to be connected at the back or side to a whole string of small buildings (the woodshed, milkhouse, etc.) terminated by a barn that tended to be much bigger than the house. However, this peculiarly New England structure originated long before the Greek Revival style. It was simply a practical farmer-created way for getting to the barn under cover when snow lay deep.

Interior treatment was basically plain but large in scale. Walls and ceilings were generally of smooth plaster. Door and window casings and baseboards were wide and edged only by simple moldings. In the fancier houses, columns on both sides of openings between the important living rooms repeated the classical character of the portico. Mantelpieces of marble or wood were essentially unornamented and stolid.

Just why Americans began to jettison the Greek Revival style when it had completed only half of its forty-year run is conjectural. Possibly the stiffness of Greek Revival was much too much for them. Undoubtedly, as the population grew and spread across the country, life was in ferment. People wanted fewer rules, less formalism. So when someone suggested that "we need to return to the romance of the medieval past", the country, led by its romantic painters and poets, began to shift its architectural course.

Andrew Jackson Downing, a landscape architect, was probably the single foremost instigator of the change. In his enormously successful book, *Cottage Residences,* published in 1842, he wrote, "I am....anxious to inspire in the minds of my readers and countrymen livelier perceptions of the BEAUTIFUL, in everything that relates to our houses and grounds." He went on to say that residential architecture should strive for three things: fitness, expression of purpose and expression of style. These he translated to mean, respectively, the beauty of utility, beauty of propriety and beauty of form and sentiment.

His ideas, illustrated with drawings and plans of a variety of "cottages" (none of which was really small; the largest of which were nearly mansions) took America by storm. The Victorian style was born in America.

Casual survey indicates that, once again, New England was not so entranced as other regions. Still, Victorian houses abound — large and small, in city and country, of every type.

To the real student of architecture, Victorian is many different styles, not one. These include, among others, the Gothic Revival style, Italian Villa, Romanesque, Italianate, Second Empire, Victorian Gothic, Queen Anne, Chateauesque, Richardsonian Romanesque, Stick style and Shingle style. If you wish to learn the particulars about these, read *A Field Guide to American Architecture* by Carole Rifkind or *What Style Is It?* published by the National Trust for Historic Preservation. I follow popular practice and label them all Victorian.

It is one style that requires no explanation. The fact that it is today enjoying a new vogue throughout the United States is ample proof of its charm. A peculiar charm, to be sure, because many Victorian houses are hideous. But behind all those towers and turrets, arched windows and gingerbread, wide eaves and steep gables there is something very appealing. And if you can afford to heat the wasted interior space, the arrangement and layout of the rooms afford a great deal of pleasant living.

As you ramble through New England looking at its thousands of old houses, several questions are likely to cross your mind:

How accurate are the dates on the houses? Relatively few are precise. In the case of the earliest houses, the dates are generally off a few years and some may be off as much as several decades. Most are usually younger than the dates indicate. But no matter. Regardless of errors in dating, regardless of how well kept up many houses are, old houses look old and are rarely to be confused with modern copies.

How much have the old houses been changed? Off-hand, I doubt that any other man-made objects change as much as houses. This, of course, is because well designed, well built, attractive houses have very long lives and have had a great many owners, most of whom had their own ideas about how the houses should be remodeled, enlarged or sometimes even reduced to suit their particular needs and to embody new equipment such as central heating plants and bathrooms. So the old house that stands today exactly as it was built is a rarity. This is particularly true of those built in the sixteen and seventeen hundreds. As was pointed out before, most of our earliest houses were very small to start with; consequently, most of them were expanded to some extent by the second or third generation of owners and then were expanded again. The ancient Fairbanks house is typical. When built in 1636 it had four rooms and measured only approximately 35 feet long and 16½ feet deep. Some years later a leanto was added across the back. Then a wing was added at one end and some time after that another wing was added at the other end. That's the way the house stands today. But in one respect the Fairbanks house is most unusual: it has never acquired modern amenities — electric lights, plumbing, heating, even a kitchen range.

What all this means, obviously, is that when we look at New England's ancient houses now, we do not get a true picture of the way they were when built. But in many cases we get a good idea; and in many other cases, we don't.

To some extent, this state of affairs is changing. Individual home owners and historical societies such as the Society for the Preservation of New England Antiquities are more and more trying to restore old houses to their early outlines. How-

ever, this almost never means going back to the house exactly as it was first built. (The Fairbanks house, for instance, will never be shorn of its leanto and wings.) The important changes and additions that were made long ago are kept because these, in many ways, are as important as the original structure. They are part of an interesting evolutionary process that should be preserved. Only the more modern "improvements" and outright excrescences are excised.

What do you call the many old houses seen in New England — as everywhere else — that do not fit neatly into any of the six major architectural styles that prevailed in the 264 years up to the Twentieth Century? They fall under the heading of vernacular architecture.

Vernacular may be defined as "of the people". One dictionary, referring specifically to architecture, defines it as "native or peculiar to popular tastes". A vernacular house, therefore, is not a professionally pure interpretation of a definite architectural style. Rather, it is strongly tinged with stylistic ideas — original, old or both — that either appeal to the local populace or that the designer thinks will appeal to his client (or to himself). It is, in short, a concoction. And like all concoctions, it is sometimes bad and sometimes good.

Where are the best old New England houses to be found? That's one of the nice things about old-house-viewing in New England: beautiful houses are everywhere. True, they thin out decidedly as you progress toward the Canadian border. They are most numerous along the coast and up the Connecticut River, because that's where the men, women and children who early settled New England congregated. But they are not restricted to the oldest and biggest cities. Many villages are chockablock with fine old houses. There are even architectural gems standing alone a good many miles out in the country.

If you feel you need a guidebook to locate the best, you can find more than one in a bookstore or through a state historical society. Or you can buy a copy of the *National Register of Historic Places* published by the National Park Service. But neither the Register nor any of the guides gives a complete picture of New England residential architecture because many of the finest old houses have for one reason or another escaped all listings.

The way to see New England houses is just to drift along the highways and byways and to poke into the centers of the towns — around the village greens and near the old churches and town halls — and look. You'll be amazed at what you find. Thrilled. And you'll discover that a substantial number of houses are open for closer inspection.

In their modest and occasionally immodest way, New England houses are as beautiful, as interesting architecturally — and often historically — as any anywhere.

Built in 1639, the Rev. Henry Whitfield house in Guilford, Conn., is the oldest stone dwelling in New England. It has been altered and realtered many times and because it is now a state-owned historical museum, it has features it did not originally possess. For example, the 55 by 15-foot "hall" stretching across the front of the house, with an enormous fireplace at each end, can now be divided by a wall that swings down from the ceiling. The wall was never in Whitfield's home, although it is an idea that was used in other ancient homes. But no matter. Much of the restored house is original, and it looks essentially like the original building — a medieval English house transplanted to very early America. The walls range from 18 to almost 30 inches thick.

BEFORE 1700

1

2

3

4

The Joshua Hempsted house was built in New London in 1678 and like the Fairbanks house opposite was enlarged several times. It was lengthened beyond the chimney by Hempsted's son and the projecting two-story wing at right in 6 — the so-called porch — was added. The windows are for the most part fixed but several have a single sash that slides into the wall — a very unusual feature. The open sash in the window at 5 is a slider.

5

6

7

Built in Dedham, Mass., in 1636, the Fairbanks house (facing page) is the country's oldest. It's still owned by the Fairbanks family but is no longer occupied. The original house, 4, had two rooms down, two rooms up and a central chimney. About thirty years later a leanto, 3, was added in back. This became the kitchen. The gambrel-roofed additions at the ends, 1 and 2, were made at different times before the end of the century. The ceilings originally were not much over 6 feet high and, because of settlement, are now so low in spots that a man cannot stand upright. The house at 7 is the Parson Capen house in Topsfield, Mass. It had two rooms on each floor from the time it was built in 1683. More on next page.

The Parson Capen house has deep overhangs in front, below the second floor, and at the ends, below the gables. These are supported at midpoint by brackets copied from the only original found when the house was restored. At the overhang ends are drops. The central chimney is pilastered; the skinny smokestack, an unhappy addition. The leaded windows, which are unusually big for such an old house, have rectangular lights (also unusual).

The Thomas Dunk house was built in 1672 in Chester, Conn. Whether it had a gambrel roof at that time is uncertain. In any case, at the other end of the house, the upper slope of the roof has been continued out over a rear leanto. Since good building stone is plentiful in this part of Connecticut, the chimney was built of it. But stone chimneys were not too common in New England. The diagonal lines across the upper sash are sticks used to "lock" the lower sash shut.

The Pond-Weed house in Darien, Conn., was built in 1695. A vertical board on the end shows where the house was extended rearwards to create a saltbox. The house was built so close to the ground that it gives no signs of having foundations. The chimney is stone.

The front part of the Wickham house in Glastonbury, Conn., was built in 1685. The side part was an addition made in 1716. Very few houses grew in this manner, for one thing — especially in this case — because a complicated restructuring of the roof was required.

The Lieut. Walter Fyler house in Windsor, Conn. (this page) had only one room when built in 1640. Capt. Nathaniel Howard, who bought it from Fyler in 1722, added a new room every time he returned from a voyage. The house now is roughly L-shaped. Opposite is the Eleazer Arnold house (1687) in Lincoln, R.I. For more, turn page.

1

2

These two houses are known as stone-enders because the chimney end was built entirely or almost entirely of stone. Such houses were peculiar to Rhode Island and nearby Massachusetts. A shrub now hides most of the stone end of the Eleazer Arnold house, but you can see how a wood addition was made above it. 2 shows the Arnold door, studded with nails in geometric pattern — a common way of decorating doors in early days. The other pictures, 3 and 4, are of the Clemence-Irons house (1680) in Johnston, R.I. Stone covers only about two-thirds of the chimney end. The catslide roof is slightly curved. The plain bargeboards under the roof are hooked at the ends.

3

4

2

3

1

28

When built in Ipswich, Mass., in 1640, the Whipple house (facing page) had on the first floor only a small entry with a great fireplace behind it and one room to the left, as in 2. It measured roughly 27 feet long by 19 deep. When first enlarged, a second bigger room was built on the other side of the entry and the chimney. From the front, the house probably looked much as in 1. Still later the two-story leanto across the back, 3, was added. The large facade gables breaking the roofline were typically Jacobean as were the end overhangs. The house displays the lack of symmetry that was characteristic of our early homes.

The Boardman house, 4, in Saugus, Mass., had four rooms — two down and two up — when built in 1687. Less then ten years later the rear roof slope was extended toward the ground to provide more space. The additions are shown by light lines on the plans. The house had a cellar under the parlor. Cellars were rare in England at the time but were widespread in New England, probably because the settlers needed a frost-free place to store food. The Boardman house has undergone a good many minor changes over the years. At one time it had facade gables like those on the Whipple house, but these were removed for some reason.

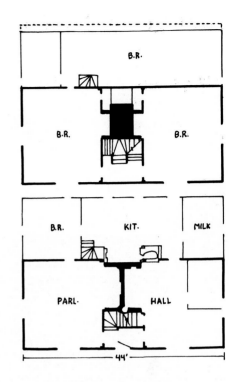

4

In 1660 the Thomas Lee house (facing page) in South Lyme, Conn., was only half as long as now. The right side was added thirty years later; and the house did not become a saltbox until 1713. By contrast, the Cooper-Frost-Austin house in Cambridge, Mass., started out in 1689 as a saltbox only one room wide. The rest of the house, beyond the chimney in the picture above, was added after 1718.

The Lee house is especially interesting because it has been thought that what is now the front was originally the back. But archeologists have recently been doing exploratory work to determine whether this is true. In any event, today's front door opens into the tiny entry shown.

The pilastered chimney top of the Cooper-Frost-Austin house was quite common in early houses and derived from the elaborate stacks on English houses. There are other examples shown in these pages.

1

2

The Hoxie house, 1 and 2, in Sandwich, Mass., was built around 1636. Although there is no obvious evidence to prove it was not built as a saltbox, it probably was not because the built-all-at-once saltbox came later in the century. Houses with leanto additions came first. The Dole-Little house, 4 and 5, in Newbury, Mass., also became a saltbox after it was built in the late 1690s. But in this case a dividing line between the original two-story structure and leanto addition is apparent. Pictures 3, 6 and 7 are of the Dole-Little house. The leaded window was typical of early windows. The wood cross-pieces behind the glass were used to strengthen the sash.

3

4

5

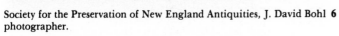
Society for the Preservation of New England Antiquities, J. David Bohl **6**
photographer.

7

The John Howland house is the last remaining Plymouth house that was occupied by actual Pilgrims. When built in 1667, it was smaller than shown at 1. The end with double-hung windows was added. The peculiar rear roofline, 2, resulted from the addition of a two-story leanto.

The Damm-Drew-Rounds house in Dover, N.H., was built in 1675. It is one of the few surviving garrison houses. Except for the large windows, it originally looked much as in picture 3, which was taken many years ago before it was moved to Dover, where it is now enclosed in a much larger protective structure at the Woodman Institute. 4 shows about as much of the exterior as the camera lens can take in. The black thing extending from the thick timber wall is a gun barrel inserted through one of the apertures used for aiming at marauding Indians. The house was only one room deep and had two big groundfloor rooms plus a small end room. The "hall" fireplace, 5, was used for cooking.

2

1

3

4

5

1

2

3

The Deacon John Moore house, 1, in Windsor, Conn., dates from 1664. The drops, 2, under the front overhang and the brackets at the ends of the second-story overhang were common on English houses and often used on New England houses. The Hyland house, 3, is in Guilford, Conn. Built in 1660, it acquired its catslide roof later. The Buttolph-Williams house, 4, was built in 1692 in Wethersfield, Conn. The eaves project more than in most houses of the period. The windows are small and few and there is none at all in the back of the house. Those in the front and sides, like those in the Hyland facade, have diamond-shaped panes set in lead. The first windows in the Moore house were undoubtedly of the same type.

1

2

3

4

5

6

7

The Stanley-Whitman house was built in Farmington, Conn., around 1667 and acquired the leanto that made it a saltbox, 8, about ninety years later. It is now a museum. Indoors, the right half is finished as in its earliest days; the left half is finished as it was roughly a century later. All pictures here are of the right half. The front door, 3 and 4, is a so-called Indian door made of vertical boards outside, horizontal boards inside. The casement windows, 5, differ from other early windows in that they were divided into two sections. 1 shows the summer beam with chamfered edges and the massive oak lintel of the huge "hall" fireplace. The corner cupboard, 2, was frequently a feature of early houses, which rarely had closets (this was true in the Colonial period, too) or other built-in storage space. The walls are paneled with wide horizontal boards.

8

Early houses were so small that they often became appendages of larger houses. That's what happened to the house at left. The right-hand wing was built in Farmington, Conn., before 1685 by William Judd. Its shed dormer is typical of our first houses. The big addition was built in 1813 by Capt. Sam Dickinson.

The Sanderson house, below, is in Lexington, Mass. It dates from 1689 but it did not look like this at that time.

When the John Ward house, right, was built in Salem, Mass., in 1684, it consisted only of the portion to the left of the door and big pilastered chimney. The right half was added within the next fifty years.

The little William Parker house, below, is in Old Saybrook, Conn. It dates from 1646. The gambrel design of the front part of the roof may have been a later alteration: gambrels were uncommon in America until the 1700s.

2   **3** M. C. Wallo.   **1**

The Bradford-Huntington house, 1, in Norwichtown, Conn., was built in two sections. The older, dating from 1659, is the smaller wing at the rear. The front part was built in 1691. Both sections were altered later. 2 shows the Hurd house, built in Woodbury, Conn., in 1680. It was a transitional house in that it combined the look of our earliest houses and the Colonial style. The Richard Gardner house, 3, is in Nantucket and was built in 1690. Since it was a saltbox to begin with, a leanto had to be added at one end to enlarge it.

Pictures 4 and 5 are of the William Peck house, built in Old Lyme, Conn., in 1666. Though it is not exactly like Cape Cod-style houses of the following century, it is very close to them and is therefore another transitional house. The peculiar stone ledge at the base of the chimney was meant to keep rain from entering the joint between chimney and roof. Flashing had not been invented at that early date. The fireplace mantel, however, is not so old as the house.

4

5

COLONIAL

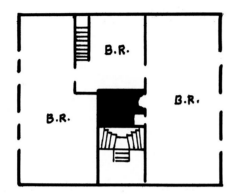

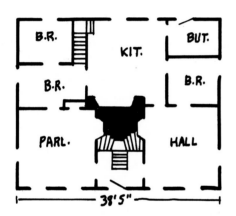

B.R.

B.R.

B.R.

B.R.

BUT.

KIT.

B.R.

B.R.

PARL.

HALL

38'5"

1

2

4096

3

The Jabez Wilder house, 1, in Hingham, Mass., is one of our best examples of the early 18th century Cape Cod house. It is also one of the prettiest. It was built about 1690; the wing to the left came later. The bow of the roof is pronounced. The doorway was originally more severe than it appears in 3: early trim was made of flat boards. The door itself is also probably not original, though the bullseye glass indicates it is plenty old. In floor plan, the house was different from many Capes in that the kitchen was sandwiched between small rooms. Ordinarily, the kitchen was much longer. This may not be the original plan, however.

As opposed to the Wilder house, which was a full Cape, the 18th Century house at 2 is a three-quarter Cape — somewhat shorter to the left of the door than to the right. It is in Cummaquid, Mass.

Collections of the Library of Congress.

46

Collections of the Library of Congress.

On the facing page are pictures of the Jabez Wilder stairway and old "hall". The stairs rise from the entry to the chimney, then split to lead to the upper bedrooms. They have come to be known as "good morning" stairs presumably because the members of the household bade one another good morning as they emerged from their bedrooms and raced to breakfast in the warm kitchen.

Above is an 18th Century half Cape in Yarmouth, Mass. Generally, in half Capes the chimney was at the doorway end of the house. Below is a corner cupboard in a Cape at North Dighton, Mass.

1

The lovely 18th Century Cape at 1 is in Madison, Conn. The wing was added. 3 is the Thomas Ash house, built in Stonington, Conn., in 1790; and 2 is a somewhat larger house of the same era in Stonington. 4 is the Peter Goodrich house in South Glastonbury, Conn. It was built in 1700. The Cape Cod style was popular in early Connecticut. Builders there were also partial to gambrel roofs, although gambrels are on Cape Cod, too. Note the second-story windows in the end of the house at 2 — two big windows flanked by two tiny ones. Frequently there was another tiny window right under the roof peak. Henry Thoreau wrote that "the great number of windows in the ends of the (Cape Cod) houses struck us agreeably — as if each of the various occupants had punched a hole where his necessities required it."

2

3 4

1

2

The John Fellows house in Mystic, Conn., at 1 is an 1826 version of the Cape Cod house. It was raised high off the ground because it was built on a hillside. The kind of tiny, gambrel-roofed house at 2 is known to people on Cape Ann, the peninsula north of Boston, as the Cape Ann cottage; but it is really only a vernacular version of the Cape Cod house. This particular house is in Rockport.

The Saconesset Homestead, 4, in West Falmouth, Mass., started out in 1678 as a bowed-roof full Cape. Later a long extension was made to the left; and still later an ell, just visible to right, was added. The Greek Revival vestibule and elaborate cornice treatment were also additions. At 3 is the woebegone Chapman-Hall house built in Damariscotta, Me., in 1755. It has almost no roof overhang in front or on the sides. The door surround is a shade more elaborate than you would expect on such a simple house but not surprising for the middle of the 18th Century.

3

4

The Samuel Webster house at East Windsor Hill, Conn., dates from 1760. It is a rather formal version of the Cape Cod house and is taller than the usual Cape because ceiling heights were gradually increased with the passing of time. The slightly projecting brick string courses in the end wall mark the floor levels. Such courses are a mark of the Georgian style of architecture, but this house is essentially Colonial.

This is the oldest house in Middletown, Conn., that still stands on its original foundations. It was built by Charles Boardman in 1753. Along with other old Colonials in the neighborhood, it has recently been done over and is now an office building. The very shallow overhangs are characteristic of many early Connecticut houses. The only explanation for them is that they relieved the stark look of the walls.

The Black Horse Tavern in Old Saybrook, Conn., was also a home (as most inns were). It was built in 1704 and has been added to. The portico and fanlight over the entrance were undoubtedly alterations. Numerous alterations were also made indoors. Even so the bedroom (upper left) is a good reflection of the house's age. The living room, right, on the other hand, is a little too elegant. This is especially true of the double-doored entrance with its curved head and the finely paneled inside shutters. Perhaps because the house was an inn, the entry is more spacious than in most Colonials. Even so, there is little space between the front door and stairs.

1

2

3

4

5

The Ebenezer Russell house, built in 1754, got a new start in life when it was recently dismantled piece by piece, moved to Lyme, Conn., and faithfully reassembled and enlarged by the addition at the rear of a big kitchen and attached garage. As a result, it is unmistakably old but lacks the imperfections that appear when a house is left for years in one place. 2 is the old parlor; 4, the old "hall"; 5, the old kitchen, now a family room. Seen through the entry, 3, and at the left side of the house, 1, is the wide coffin door that many early homes had. The need for it is apparent when you consider how difficult it would be to maneuver a coffin through the narrow entry and out the front door without standing it on end.

1

2

Although this house was built before 1798, it owes its shape and appearance to Joseph Arnold, who purchased it in that year and expanded it in every direction to hold his twelve children. It is now known by the name of his wife, Thankful Arnold. It's in Haddam, Conn. A very simple place outside and in, it's distinguished by the bell-shaped gambrel roof. Built into a hillside, it is a tall three stories in front, 1, and two stories in back, 2.

The facade of the Osborn house, 5, in Southport, Conn., is out of balance. This was rare in a house built in 1734 but not in earlier houses. The windows in Picture 3 are in a Newport home. They project about two inches and have no casings. This is because the walls were sheathed with vertical planks and were only about three inches thick, so if the window frames were to be flush with the interior wall surface, they had to stick out in the other direction. The window at 4 is in the Platts-Bradstreet house, built in Rowley, Mass., in 1660. An 18th Century replacement for an early leaded window, it shows how thick wood muntins were in the Colonial era.

3   4

5

The Stephen Mather house, 2, was built in Darien, Conn., in 1778. Although the little portico was added, the house is exactly what most of us visualize when the New England Colonial architectural style is mentioned. The double-hung windows have nine lights over six. The doorway, 1, in the Capt. Thomas Newson house, built in Wethersfield, Conn., in 1710, is wider and a bit more elaborate than most Colonial entrances. The Caleb Stone house, 3, in Guilford, Conn., began life as a saltbox in 1749; then a leanto was added. The result is an unusually long, flaring catslide. The Fairfield, Conn., house at 4 is dated only as "pre-Revolutionary". A leanto addition was made at some time. No attempt was made to align its first-floor window with that in the original house.

1

2

3

4

The Jared Leete house, above, in Guilford, Conn. was built in 1774. Whoever added the leanto at the back did so with a fine eye for appearances. It ties into the main body of the house almost as well as if it were under a catslide roof. But the very recent addition of bay windows on the front of the house nearly spoils everything. The 1820 house in Norwich, Vt., at right, is built of brick and has end chimneys but it is still essentially of the Cape Cod style. Many of the Capes built in the first half of the 19th Century deviated considerably from the basic style — just as modern Capes do.

The Rev. James Lockwood's house was built in Wethersfield, Conn., in 1767. It is a substantial gambrel-roofed structure to which a rear wing was later added; and as a parson's house should, it made no show (most Wethersfield houses did not). The portico and over-window treatment are very simple. The double door is surmounted by a large semicircular fanlight. This was the most common form of fanlight until the 1800s. Elliptical fanlights came into use a little before 1800 and, along with segmental fanlights, really took over after that. But they eventually succumbed to the long, rectangular transom lights that characterized the Greek Revival style.

GEORGIAN

1

2

3

4

The Gov. Meshech Weare house, 1, was built in Hampton Falls, N.H., in 1723. The Deacon Joseph Denison house, 2, is in Stonington, Conn. It dates from 1730. The small addition at the left of the Denison place was recently made and is in perfect keeping with the old house. The Parson Ashley house, 3, is in Deerfield, Mass. Built in 1730, it was later moved and used as a tobacco barn for 75 years before it was returned to its site and reconstructed. Pictures of its magnificent door are on the next pages. 4 is the Rev. John Sergeant house, built in 1739 in Stockbridge, Mass. Its door is shown overleaf, too.

Early builders knew one thing that modern builders have never learned: a pretty doorway can turn a plain-Jane house into a Cinderella. Doorways throughout New England demonstrate this. But nowhere are the doorways so distinctive as on the Georgian houses in the Connecticut River Valley. No one knows why this came to be. But it was a recognized fact almost from the start of the Georgian period and homeowners elsewhere in New England often hired Valley joiners to make their doorways.

The scroll-pedimented doorway is the most famous of Valley designs but it was just one of several that were used. Very few of these remain on the houses for which they were built. Here are two; others appear elsewhere in this book. Above is the doorway on the Sergeant house in Stockbridge. At right and across the page is that on the Ashley house in Deerfield. They look almost identical but close study will show that they are not. All surviving scroll pediment doorways are different to some degree.

Above was briefly the home of John Paul Jones and is now generally known by his name. But it was built in Portsmouth in 1758 by Capt. Gregory Purcell, a merchant sea captain. The other three pictures are of the Sheldon-Hawks house built in Deerfield in 1743. The door and window treatments of the two houses are interesting to compare. The Jones house has a segmental pedimented doorway and triangular pediments over the windows whereas triangular pediments were used on both the door and windows of the Sheldon house. The latter, incidentally, are thought to have been added some years after the house was put up, and in the process a double door with very narrow 21-inch leaves was substituted for a single door. Note that in both houses the second-story windows have no pediments because the windows are close under the eaves.

1

2

3

4

Here are three handsome saltbox houses. The Babcock-Smith house on the facing page was built in Westerly, R.I., in 1732. It has a gambrel roof, 3, and the projecting porch, as it was called in the old days, has a scroll-pedimented doorway. 4 shows the Thomas Griswold house in Guilford, Conn. It dates from 1774 and has a noticeably steeper roof, especially in front, than the other houses. The Dudley house, built in Madison, Conn., in 1740, is at 5.

1

2

Newport boasts one of the finest collections of ancient houses in New England or anywhere else. The work going on to restore them is outstanding. 3 shows a typical street scene. At 4 is the Nathan Day house in East Windsor Hill, Conn. It dates from 1734. 1 and 2 are of the Ely house, built in Chester, Conn., in 1787. It is a splendid example of a medium-size Georgian house, with quoins at the corners, a fine doorway and portico, window pediments and ornamental cornice. The tooth-like blocks are modillions. Cut-stone foundations like these are common in areas where good quarry stone abounds. They are too handsome to be hidden behind shrubbery.

3

4

Brick and stone have never been widely used in New Englad houses although brick homes are plentiful enough. Stone homes like the Fay-Brown dwelling (below), built in Old Bennington, Vt., in 1781 by the local tavern-keeper, are rare. Also rather rare are houses like the Short house, left. It has brick ends but is clapboarded front and back. It was built in Newbury, Mass., in 1733. Opposite is the Capt. Elisha White house, put up in 1750 in Clinton, Conn. Above the windows the bricks are laid in an arched soldier (upright) course. Floor levels are marked by string courses.

The Elijah Burt house (directly opposite) in East Long-meadow, Mass., would be an ordinary two-story Colonial if the door and windows were stripped of their pediments, but these features make it a Georgian. It was built in 1720. Above the Burt house is the Harrington house in Weston, Mass. Note that the latter has shutters, the former does not. Shutters did not come into general use until the late 1700s. Many houses have never had them. In any case, those on the Harrington house are fairly new because early louvered shutters had much larger slats. On this page is the Crown-inshield-Bentley house, built in Salem, Mass., around 1727. There is some evidence that it started out as a half house and was twice expanded. The tall, compact ell on the left side is a Beverly jog, presumably so named because it was first used in nearby Beverly, Mass. The roof of a jog follows the roofline of the body of the house.

All pictures except one on these pages are of the Dwight-Barnard house in Deerfield. It was built in Springfield in 1725, became a tenement house, and was finally moved to Deerfield in the 1950s by Mr. and Mrs. Henry N. Flynt, who were mainly responsible for the restoration of this ancient village and founded Historic Deerfield. That the house was well worth saving is obvious. At far, bottom right is the doorway of the Thomas Hayden house (1767) in Windsor, Conn. Without the storm-screen door it would be even handsomer. But, alas, storm and screen doors and windows are ever with us in New England.

Even for New England, where houses have been changed time after time, the Hooper-Lee-Nichols house in Cambridge has undergone an amazing metamorphosis. Today it stands as a big Georgian house with some Federal features, such as the roof balustrade. But as the drawings by M. David Samson, resident fellow for the Cambridge Historical Society, show, it started out in 1685 as a Jacobean house (the window placement and size to the right of the door are conjectural), became a Colonial about 1717, and then took on the Georgian style about 1735. Somewhere along the way the ends of the house were built of masonry. One of the astonishing features of the present house is the front door, which is over four feet wide but of only normal height.

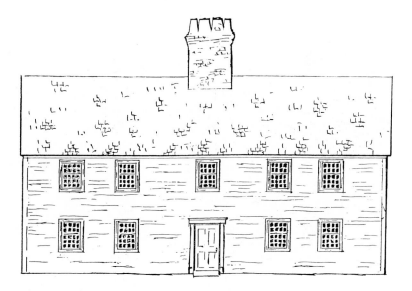

The Winslow Crocker house in Yarmouthport, on Cape Cod, looks as if it belongs to the Cape. Though larger than the great majority of old Cape Cod homes, it is shingled like them and has the same spare, weathered look. But the triangular pedimented doorway and window cornices spell it out as of the Georgian style, and originally it had a typical Georgian floor plan. It was constructed in 1780 in nearby West Barnstable and during its long lifetime there it was more or less split down the middle by a partition so that Crocker's two sons and their families could live in it together. In 1935, however, it was uprooted, moved to its present site, restored, given a modern kitchen (not that shown) and bathrooms, and donated to the Society for the Preservation of New England Antiquities, which today opens it to the public throughout the summer.

Society for the Preservation of New England Antiquities, J. David Bohl photographer.

The fireplace at left is in the 1759 home of Jonathan Warner, of Hadlyme, Conn. It is not the largest kitchen fireplace in New England: some were big enough to walk into. But it is early Georgian period. Like most of these fireplaces, it had a built-in oven (oven placement varied from the front of the fireplace to the back of the firebox itself). The paneling is simple but the width of the boards makes it gorgeous.

The Samuel Tenney house in Exeter, N.H., is of unusual design. The central three bays are three stories high while the outer bays are only two stories. This permitted windows to be installed in the clerestory, thus greatly improving the natural lighting and ventilation of the third floor. The house was built in 1800. The Doric columns framing the doorway support a classic Doric entablature and a pediment. The tympanum (area within the pediment) is decorated with wooden tracery. The first-story windows have cornices while those in the second story are topped with keystones.

On the opposite page is the Capt. Amos Palmer house in Stonington, Conn. Built high above the street in 1780, it is approached by graceful curving steps.

1

2

The Williams College president's house (1801) at Williamstown, Mass., is typical of the great Georgian mansions although not so large as many. The handsome facade, 1, with quoins at the corners and Ionic pilasters setting off the bays, 2, has a large, beautiful doorway surmounted by a very large Palladian window under a deep cornice and wide ornamented panel in the roof balustrade. Even the friezes below the window cornices, 3, are decorated.

4 shows the much simpler but lovely doorway of the John Calder house in Providence. It dates from 1759.

3

4

1

More Connecticut River Valley doorways. 1 — Ebenezer Grant, East Windsor Hill, Conn., 1722. 2 — Rev. Ebenezer Gay, 1795, Suffield, Conn. 3 — John Dickinson, about 1762, Hatfield, Mass. 4 — also in Hatfield, 1700. 5 — Deerfield, middle 1700s. Compare the last two — so alike yet differing in small details.

2

3

4

5

The Hart house (opposite page, top) was built in Old Saybrook, Conn., in 1767. The Welles-Shipman-Ward house (this page) is in South Glastonbury, Conn., and dates from 1755. At a glance they look much alike, as many New England houses do. The Hart house has more of the Colonial severity but has end chimneys. The Welles house, on the other hand, is of Colonial plan, has a big central chimney and 9½ by 4½-foot kitchen fireplace, but is much more highly ornamented. The 18th Century house at bottom, facing page, is one of a number of fine old houses that might have been demolished if space had not been cleared for them on The Hill in Portsmouth. Most of the houses are now used for commercial purposes.

The Dalton house, this page, was built in Newburyport, Mass., in 1746. It is one of the city's larger houses but not one of its most ostentatious. The doorway is handsome. The treatment of the dormers, which are neatly aligned with the windows below, is typically Georgian. Four of the windows are topped by triangular pediments; the center has a broken pediment.

The College Hill area of Providence has been called one of the most beautiful city residential areas to be found in the United States. This is a tribute more to the Hill's houses than to anything else. The doorways and adjacent facade areas are notable. The facade of the William Ashton house (1790) on the facing page is particularly delightful even though fanciful.

The Capt. Samuel Mather house (opposite, top) was built in Old Lyme, Conn., about 1784. Like most New England Georgian houses, it is clapboarded. The Wentworth-Gardner house (left) in Portsmouth, on the other hand, has clapboards on the sides and V-jointed horizontal flush siding in front. The Vernon house in Newport (above) looks as if made of stone but the stones are really boards. The Wentworth-Gardner house has the same vertical grooves but they're not noticeable. The houses date from 1760 and 1758.

Tombstone paneling like that in a bedroom of the Selden house (facing page) was rare in Georgian houses despite its beauty. Many experts consider this among the finest in the country. Which doesn't mean that there is anything second-rate about the parlor paneling (right). The fireplaces are also unusual and beautiful. But the arches are directly exposed to flame and that at right has been charred.

There is considerable evidence that the Selden house in Hadlyme, Conn., started life in 1693 in the small gambrel-roofed wing behind the main body. Of course at that time the lower slope of the front roof did not curve gracefully out over a porch and small room, which have been added. The big Georgian addition was made in the 1700s after the original house was almost razed by fire.

All Americans own this famous house in Cambridge. It is known as the Longfellow house because the poet lived here for years. But it was built in 1759 by Henry Vassall and the piazzas and other additions were built by Andrew Craigie before Longfellow moved in. Today it is the property of the National Park Service and you can visit it and its beautiful grounds almost any time. It ranks as one of our truly great Georgian homes.

1

The Victorian furnishings of the Long-fellows tend to obscure the fact that the rooms are Georgian. Note the stairway, 1, the cornices, 2, the treatment of the fire-place end of the parlor, 4. Longfellow's study is at 5; the fireplace with later-added tiles, 3, is in one of the bedrooms.

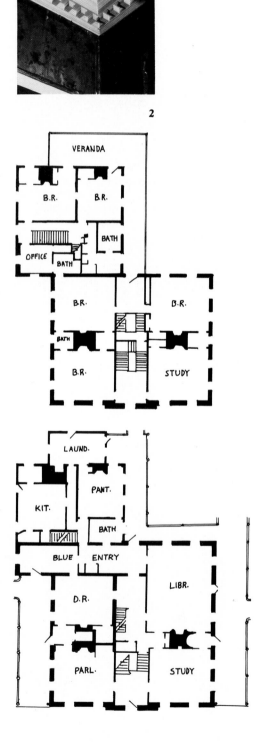

2

3

4

5

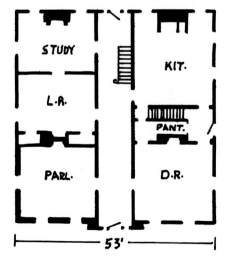

Here are two of the great houses on College Hill in Providence. The Nightingale (1792) is on the facing page; the John Brown house (1786) here. The former is wood; the latter, brick. Both are gorgeously ornamented outside and in. John Quincy Adams called the Brown house "the most magnificent and elegant private mansion that I have seen on the continent". Both have pavilions (slightly projecting center bays) with quite different but equally fine Palladian windows.

The Jonathan Warner house above was built in
Chester, Conn., in 1798. It is essentially a large but
simple Colonial with a great many fine Georgian
details accented by the columned pavilion. Strictly
speaking, what appears to be a Palladian window
is not one. It is actually three round-topped windows. This puts it under the heading of a vernacular version of the real thing. At right is the Tap-
ping-Reeve house (1773) in Litchfield, Conn. The
facade has little embellishment but the deep framing of the windows is effective because it produces
a shadowbox look. The grilles in the frieze are
ventilators for the low attic.

The Hatheway house (1736) in Suffield, Conn., seems to look far larger in actuality than in the pictures. With the Dutch Colonial addition to its left end, it stretches for miles. Big or little, it is a beauty owned, like several other houses in this book, by the Antiquarian and Landmarks Society, in Hartford, and is open to the public. The two front entrances differ considerably, indicating that they were probably constructed at different times. The large one with portico is quite plain while that in the wing has a fanlight and sidelights. The windowheads consist of a molded, dentilled entablature with convex frieze.

1

The Salisbury Mansion, 1, 3 and 4, was built in Worcester in 1772. The flush board siding under the portico was being scraped when these pictures were taken. The effect created by the modillions on the cornice and large pediment is repeated on a smaller scale by dentils under the window cornices.

The portico and roof balustrades differ. Compare the latter with the extremely simple roof balustrade of the Ropes Mansion, which was built in Salem, Mass., in the late 1720s. Because the Salisbury roof is hipped, the balustrade is level all the way around. On the Ropes house, the balustrade follows the gambrel roof slopes.

3

4

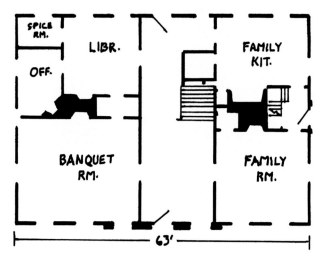

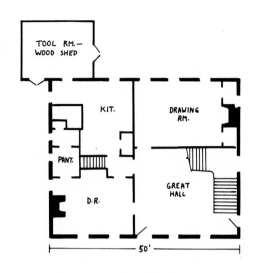

Two of the great New England mansions: The Col. Jeremiah Lee house, in Marblehead, Mass., at left; the Moffatt-Ladd house, Portsmouth, on this page. The former was built in 1768; the latter, five years earlier. The first-floor plans differ decidedly. The Moffatt-Ladd entrance hall is unusual in its monumentality. The Lee house has a charming cupola, rusticated board siding and a pavilion. The Moffatt-Ladd house has an airily graceful rooftop balustrade, flush board siding and no pavilion. The over-window treatment in the Lee house is uniform; the Moffatt-Ladd house has segmental pediments over the first-floor windows and scroll pediments over those in the second story.

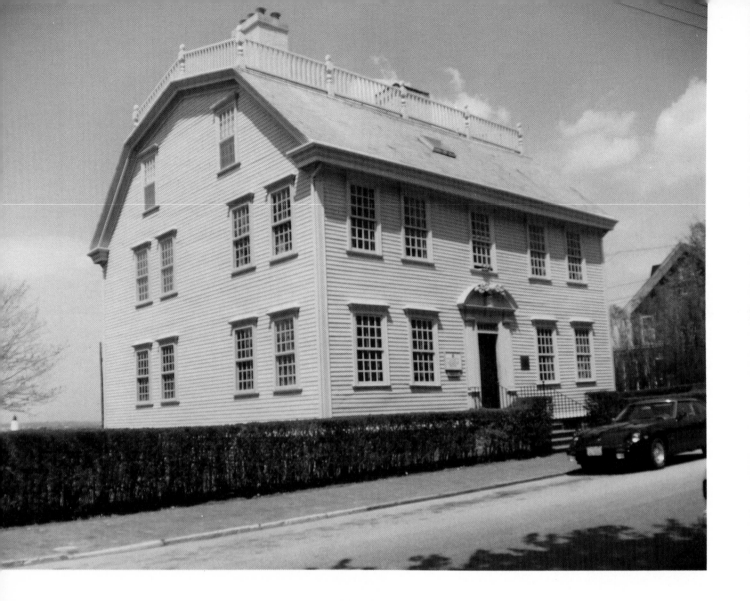

The Hunter house above speaks for itself. It is considered the outstanding early house in Newport, and in Newport that's saying a lot. It was built around 1746. The smallish 18th Century house at left is tucked away on the waterfront in Salem, Mass. The surrounding commercial buildings are so drab that you're discouraged from looking for it. Also in Salem is the Peirce-Nichols house, dating from 1782. It is thought to have been Samuel McIntire's first major commission. Whether true or not, it is one of his finest works. The low-pitched roof is hidden by the balustrade, which also obscures a second balustrade encircling a small roof deck. The huge fluted corner pilasters are the main ornamental feature of the facade, which is broken by the simple window cornices and the shadows they cast. Like the pilasters, the portico is essentially of the Doric order. The interiors were remodeled by McIntire in 1801 and combine the Georgian and Federal styles.

These three houses comprise the Webb-Deane-Stevens Museum in Wethersfield, Conn. The Silas Deane house (1766) is above and close by to its right is the Joseph Webb house (1752) followed by the Isaac Stevens house (1788), both shown below. Shown on the facing page are the hall and parlor in the Deane house. Note particularly the balusters and scrollwork. The doorway is to the Webb house. The museum is owned by the National Society of the Colonial Dames of America in Connecticut.

Interiors by John Giammatteo.

113

The Wells-Thorn house (facing page) is in Deerfield. The fortress-like rear wing was built in 1717; the sky-blue front section, in 1751. The Wentworth-Coolidge house (this page) on the outskirts of Portsmouth comes as a shock when you first see it. It is very, very odd — big and rambling with no easily ascertainable style and with a big shed-roof piece jutting into the air as on an ultra-modern house. But in a short time, you begin to find it attractive. It is certainly one of New England's most interesting homes. More on the following pages.

1

There is some thought that the Wentworth-Coolidge house was an assemblage of ancient warehouses moved to the site. True or not, it has grown in strange fashion, as the plan shows. Section B was the start in the early 1700s. Its gloomy interior bespeaks its age. (A is a modern caretaker's wing.) Then about 1750 came C, more Colonial. 5 shows a bedroom in this area. Then D, the parlor shown at 1, and E, Governor Wentworth's council chamber with its magnificent fireplace, 3 and 4, were built after 1753. This is the Georgian heart of the house and from the entrance hall, 2, inward, it is very handsome. Finally F, a guest wing, was added by the Coolidges in the present century. The house today is the property of the State of New Hampshire. It is sparsely furnished; donations are being sought. But it is fascinating in the way it rambles up, down and around, and in its odd mixture of architecture.

116

2

3

4

5

The Hezekiah Chaffee house (facing page) was built in Windsor, Conn., in 1765. The rear wing, which was used either as a countinghouse or to house slaves, and a small wing at the right end, which was Chaffee's office, were built with it. The string courses indicating floor levels stand out prominently. Note that they do not run the entire length of the walls — a typically Georgian quirk. On this page is the Codman house in Lincoln, Mass. Built between 1735 and 1741, it was originally a two-story L-shaped Georgian dwelling. In 1797 it was vastly enlarged to imitate an English country home. The shutters on the pedimented windows are of the thick heavy type first used. No one agrees whether the louvers on such shutters should slant up or down.

Society for the Preservation of New England Antiquities, Richard Cheek photographer.   **1**

The interior of the Codman house was altered twice after the major remodeling in 1797; consequently, it now has Georgian, Federal, Victorian and Classical Revival features. The stairs, 1, are Georgian. The dining room, 2, is Elizabethan Revival.

120

2

3

The Jabez Bacon house was built in Woodbury, Conn., in 1760. A large gambrel-roofed structure with the slight overhangs favored in Connecticut and a central chimney, it is plain but made handsome by its door-

way, 3. On the Ebenezer King house, 4, the doorways are prominent but the entire house, including the wing added at the rear, displays Georgian elegance. The house was built in Suffield, Conn., in 1795.

4

The Julius Deming house is in Litchfield, Conn. When built in 1793, it looked more like one of the foursquare houses along the seacoast. Then it was remodeled to look like this. Despite the considerable height of the house and the imposing pavilion, the house appears lower than it is because of the strong line created by the cornices over the windows and portico and because of the width of the pavilion. The roof balustrade also contributes to this feeling because it has no intermediate posts.

The Gov. John Langdon house in Portsmouth should be viewed in winter when it isn't partially concealed by trees. But behind its handsome fence, it stands out clearly enough in summer to tell you that this is a gorgeous place. It was built in 1784. The Chinese Chippendale roof balustrade is unique. The dormer roofs have an unusually wide overhang, are ornamented with modillions (as is the main cornice) and are crowned by unusually ornate pediments. The house was altered several times but the main change was made in 1906 when the old kitchen wing was removed in favor of a new wing with an elegant large dining room, kitchen and second-floor bedrooms.

The John Langdon
house has been des-
cribed as a bit florid in
comparison with other,
mostly earlier Georgian
houses. Be that as it may,
the interiors shown
here, like the exterior,
are magnificent. The
new dining room was
designed by architect
Stanford White and was
modeled on the Federal
dining room in another
Portsmouth house. As
noted by the Society for
the Preservation of New
England Antiquities,
which now owns the
house, "it combines the
delicate coloring and
decoration of both the
original Langdon din-
ing room and White's
work in the White
House in Washington."

Society for the Preservation of New England Antiquities, J. David Bohl photographer.

The Samuel Barnard house (this page) was built in Deerfield in 1768. It was and still is unusually elegant for this old town. The doorway with its modillioned segmental-arched pediment sets the tone for the entire house.

The Hamilton house is so hidden in the South Berwick, Me., hills that you wonder why it was ever built there. But in 1785, the river below the bluff on which the house stands was alive with traffic and wharves and warehouses crowded the shores. Then as now the house could not fail to attract attention. The front is at the top of the opposite page; the back, at the bottom. Scroll-pediment dormers are centered between simpler broken-pediment dormers.

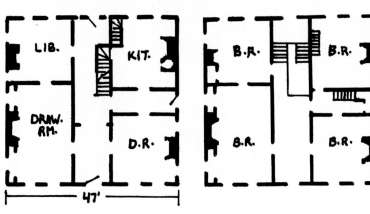

Society for the Preservation of New England Antiquities, Douglas Armsden photographer.

The Hamilton house stairway (facing page) is flooded with light from the arched window on the landing. The size of the window is less apparent here than in the preceding picture of the front of the house. On this page is the Pearson house, built in 1798 in Poppersquash, R.I. It is the kind of house you wish you owned yourself, but because of the wings added to the side and back, it is larger than it looks.

FEDERAL

It is fitting that the Gardner-Pingree house (1804) in Salem, Mass., opens the Federal architecture chapter because it's one of the finest Federals in the town that is considered to be one of the great, if not the greatest, centers of Federal architecture. That's because of Samuel McIntire, a Salem native. He probably designed the Gardner-Pingree house, certainly did the doorway and portico with its Corinthian columns and pilasters. The house itself is beautifully proportioned. The windows are rhythmically placed. The red-brown string courses, stretching to the wall ends (as in Federal design) emphasize both the horizontal and vertical proportions of the house. The balustrade hides the low-pitched hip roof.

On the facing page is the Samuel Ely house, built in Lyme, Conn., in 1750. It is one of New England's most exquisite Georgian homes. The wing behind the house is older than the main body; the section attached to it is modern.

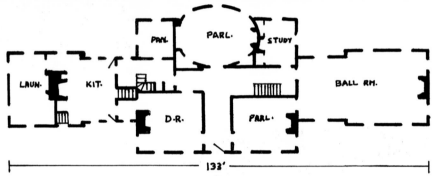

|←————————— 133' —————————→|

These two incredible houses in Waltham, Mass., were Federal-style trend-setters although many of their features were taken from earlier Federals. The Lyman house, on this page, was built in 1793. Samuel McIntire was the architect. The larger Gore Place dates from 1805. It is attributed to Charles Bulfinch. Both houses have the large projecting elliptical rooms that were popular in Federal architecture. In the Gore house note how some of the windows were lengthened to floor level. That was a new Federal idea that Bulfinch particularly favored.

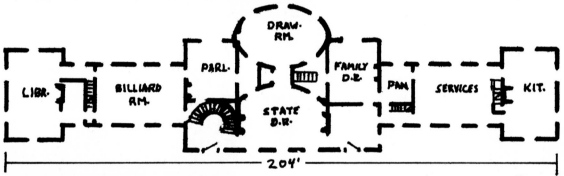

LIBR. BILLIARD RM. PARL. DRAW. RM. FAMILY D.R. PAN. SERVICES KIT.

STATE D.R.

204'

The Beacon Hill section of Boston is one of the best areas in which to see prime Federal architecture. Of course, the houses are for the most part jammed close to their neighbors. Some are large; some, small. But all are interesting and attractive.

In large part, this concentration of beauty is attributable to Charles Bulfinch, one of the United States' foremost architects. He did not design all the houses but he was responsible for many — partly because he undertook to build several developments that eventually forced him into bankruptcy. For a time thereafter he served as chairman of Boston's board of selectmen and police superintendent. But he culminated his career by completing the Capitol in Washington.

Left side of famed Louisburg Square, built from 1834 to 1848. Some houses have flat fronts; others are bowed.

Bulfinch designed Nos. 13, 15 and 17 Chestnut St. The first two are shown here.

House at 29A Chestnut St. is set perpendicular to the street and faces a side garden. A common practice.

The David Sears house (1814), Beacon St. The left side was added in 1832; the third floor, in 1875.

The Nathan Appleton house (1818), Beacon St. The fourth floor was added seventy years later.

Small second-story balconies were popular on Beacon Hill. You stepped out on them through long windows.

Stephen Higginson house (1804), Mt. Vernon St. Bulfinch put door off center to improve the living space.

The little town of Castleton, Vt., has a remarkable collection of houses designed in most part by a native son, Thomas R. Dake. Dake based his designs on the standard styles and added his own ideas. One of his works was the Harris house, 1, built in 1820. Here he used a modillioned cornice over a garlanded frieze, his own idea of a Palladian window and Federal doorway. The panes in the window and doorway sidelights flaw an otherwise attractive house. In and around Old Bennington, Vt., architects and builders enjoyed arching the heads of the three windows in their Palladian windows. 2 is a closeup of the door and window in the house at 3. 4 is a white-brick Federal in Wiscasset, Me., which is noted for its fine homes.

136

3

4

1

2

Even without a balustrade to conceal it, the roof of the Samuel Davis house, 1, in Kennebunkport, Me., is hidden. But the chimneys, as on most Federal houses, stand tall and slim. 2 is a large brick house at Center Harbor, N.H. It has been enlarged by wings since it was built in 1800. 3 is the Isaac Vose house in Milton, Mass. It was built in 1785. The Taylor-Barry house, 4, was built in Kennebunk, Me., in 1803 and added to later.

138

3

4

Facing the Salem, Mass., common is the monumental brick Andrew-Safford house, built in 1819. The columned portico towers above the street; the three-section window above is crowned by a wood fan within a larger arch. A great porch and balcony overlook the garden. The roof balustrade is broken by panels containing fans. A smaller balustrate surrounds the deck at the roof peak. Opposite is one of Samuel McIntire's beautiful porticoed doorways. It is from the Gideon-Tucker house, which is no more. It's now on the back of the Essex Institute.

The Sophia Bissell Haskell house and the Aaron Bissell house (this page) stand side by side in East Windsor Hill, Conn. They are virtually identical. Aaron Bissell built them in 1813 and 1812 respectively. Facing page: King Caesar II was the name that Duxbury, Mass., residents gave to Ezra Weston, Jr., and this is the King Caesar house, built in 1798. It is a home worthy of a rich shipbuilder and banker. Today the doorway, unfortunately flanked by downspouts, looks worn but beautiful anyway. The lead tracery of the fanlight and sidelights is outstanding even for the Federal period, when it was used freely and gracefully.

The Cushing house is one of the more conservative big four-square captain's houses in Newburyport, Mass. It was built in 1808. There is little to distinguish one side from the other except that the front door has sidelights and the window above it is arched. The bottom picture shows the side facing a fragrant old rose garden.

Tiny New Ipswich, N.H., hardly seems the proper location for the mansion opposite; but it was built there in 1800 by Charles Barrett as a wedding present for his son because that's where the family lived and made its fortune. The tremendously long carriage house to the left was part of the original house. The unusual doorway in the pavilion has blind panels above the sidelights and fanlight. The fanlight in the pediment is scalloped around the edge. Note the panels alternating with balusters in the roof balustrade — a Federal characteristic. A ballroom extends across the entire front of the house on the third floor.

1

2

3

4

5

The Cushman house, 1, in eastern Vermont was built in 1795. It has been owned for many years by an artist who, among other things, built a large addition at the right and lengthened the first-floor windows overlooking a lovely garden in the rear, 2. But the decorative features, such as the graceful urns on the upper corners of the Palladian window, 5, and the fanlight, 3, are original. The artist did, however, color the rosettes alternating with diamonds in the archivolt. It was an inspired idea. 4 is a large pink brick 19th Century house in Woodstock, Vt. The portico and doorway are very wide. The recessed blind arches above the first-floor windows are an adaptation of a Bulfinch-favored feature seen on other houses.

One of the architectural sights of New England is The Ridge in Orford, N.H. Here, strung out in a long row on a hillside about a hundred yards-back from the fences along the highway are seven beautiful houses built from 1804 to 1839 (in reality, the middle house was begun in 1773, but its main body was not constructed till 1804). The house shown at right is the northernmost in the row and was built in 1828 by William Howard. It is probably the most imposing of the group and is much larger than it looks at the end of its manicured lawn, because it has a long ell in back.

Above is the Emerson house in Norwich, Vt. Built in 1815, it displays in its doorway and friezes below the roof and window cornices the delicate but extravagant ornamentation that Vermonters seem to have doted on at that time. House after house makes a similar show.

Stone houses tend to have a massive look and the Deshon-Allyn house, built in New London in 1829, does not disappoint in this respect. But it also has a prettiness that impresses the viewer far more than its solidity. This stems largely from the arched windows in the dormers and the very lovely Palladian window, which is recessed slightly in its stone frame. The bold delineation of the doorway and windows is a Greek Revival characteristic, as is the rectangular transom over the door. But on the whole, the house belongs to the Federal period. There are few like it elsewhere.

The Gov. Blaine house (opposite, top) was built in Augusta, Me., in the 1830s. Presumably by this time Federal architecture had given way to Greek Revival; but it must be remembered that style changes almost always lagged in the hinterlands, and Augusta was then back country. Be that as it may, the governor was ahead of his time a bit in building a Victorian cupola. The Deacon Ezra Southworth house (opposite, bottom) was built in Deep River, Conn., in 1840 out of stone quarried on the site. If stripped of its porch and facade gable, it belongs to the Federal era.

1

3

The Perry-Dudley house, 1, was built in Exeter, N.H., in 1818. The Gardner house, 2, is next door and dates from 1826. The two bear a strong resemblance although details differ. In both cases, the porticoes were additions.

2

The Parsonage in Hollis, N.H., was built in 1813. From its brick ends, 4, rise towering chimneys. The doorway, 3, is like a Palladian window set in a clapboarded facade. The Meacham-Ainsworth house in Castleton, Vt., is hardly identifiable as a Federal house because architect Thomas Dake put into it a dash of this, a dash of that. But the front portico, 5, is delightful, decorated like the frieze beneath the cornice with Dake's beloved garlands. The triangular ventilator in the side gable, 6, gives the illusion of having deep triangular pockets but is really just flaw and louvered.

4

5

6

1

M. C. Wallo.

2

3

The John W. Barrett house, 1, in Nantucket was constructed sometime before 1846. It was raised high off the ground, perhaps to improve the sea view from the large enclosed cupola. This, of course, required the curving steps up to the landing of the rather heavy-looking portico. Like the roof balustrades in so many Federal houses, this one has big panels alternating with sets of balusters. The Thomas Macy II house, 2, is also in Nantucket. Built in 1770, it was enlarged in 1827. The beautiful entrance is topped by a wood fan surrounded by a fringe suggesting an embroidery chain. The triple window was a Federal development.

154

4

Nantucket is the home of many fine old houses of all sizes, shapes and styles. The Three Bricks, 3, are not the best but they come close to dominating the town. They were built from 1836 to 1838 by Joseph Starbuck for his three sons and are known as East Brick, Middle Brick and West Brick. They are peas in a pod. The porticoes, 4, are identical. Perhaps because they were built and evidently designed by a carpenter and mason, the houses don't have the architectural purity an architect might have given them. They've been described as Georgian, Greek Revival as well as Federal.

1

A collection of Federal doorways. 1 — the Gardner house (1806) in Providence. 2 — the Harriet Beecher Stowe house (1804) in Brunswick, Me. The doorway itself is heavy and Greek Revival in feeling. The door with its fanciful panels and surrounding flowered stained-glass lights is the interesting feature. 3 — a Providence doorway circa 1795. Providence abounds in beautiful doorways. 4 — the entrance to the Francis Parkman house (1830s) in Boston is at right. Its neighbor is lovely, too. They are tied together by the window, with a fanlight more or less like the neighbor's and sidelights like both. 5 — another recessed doorway up the street from the Parkman house. 6 — an 1823 doorway in Belfast, Me. The incomplete pilasters beside the door are odd.

2

3

4

5

6

An 1800 house in Thomaston, Me. This is a fine example of how an otherwise plain house is transformed by a good doorway and, in this case, the hall window above. The window construction is unusual: rarely is a double-hung window framed by a fanlight and sidelights.

Probably New England's most unusual kind of structure is the house connected to the barn by one or more small buildings used as a woodshed, milkhouse, etc. This is not found in any other part of the country; and except for a few rarities is found only in northern New England. At left is an example in Jaffrey, N.H. The big barn is downhill from and behind the house, which was built in 1804 and is hidden by trees. The two are connected by a shed-roofed building serving various purposes.

Society for the Preservation of New England Antiquities, J. David Bohl photographer.

Harrison Gray Otis, a lawyer, congressman, and mayor of Boston, built three Federal houses in Boston. All were designed by Charles Bulfinch. This was the first, erected at 141 Cambridge Street in 1796. It is now the headquarters of the Society for the Preservation of New England Antiquities. One of the earlier of Bulfinch's numerous houses, it reflects the proportions and delicate details of which he was a master but it lacks the ideas that made him a pacesetter. The plan follows Georgian precedent. The kitchen ell was originally one story high but is now three. At left is the front hall.

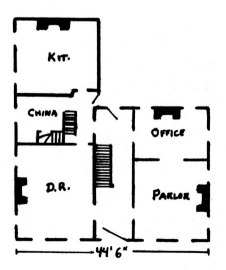

In a lesser house, the detailing would be pretty consistent throughout. But in the first Harrison Gray Otis house, Bulfinch showed great variety, as is to be seen especially in the mantelpieces and cornices.

Society for the Preservation of New England Antiquities, J. David Bohl photographer.

The second Harrison Gray Otis house (opposite) was built in 1802 at 85 Mt. Vernon St. The front faces the street but the entrance, originally on the west side, was relocated and is now at the back right corner. The facade is more classical than that of the first Otis house. The windows of the first-floor parlors extend to the floor and are set in the recessed blind arches Bulfinch liked. On this page is the third Otis house, built at 45 Beacon St. in 1808. It is the biggest of the three houses. The main living areas were on the second floor, shown in plan. Here triple-hung windows opened from the front rooms onto Chinese fretwork balconies.

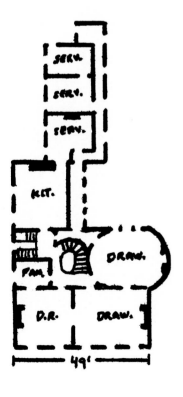

1

2   3   4

The Merwin house, 1,
called Tranquility, was
built in Stockbridge,
Mass., in 1825. Like a fair
number of Federals,
especially in the colder
parts of New England, it
was of brick, but it was
extended near the end of
the century by a Shingle-
style ell. The doorway, 4,
with a masonry surround
sort of like an Egyptian
headdress, is now locked
and treated as a window.
The other pictures are of
the Nickels-Sortwell
house. Its marvelous
elliptical staircase, 6, is
lighted by a skylight, 3,
and an unusual half-
round window, 5.2 is one
of its handsome door-
ways. The carving
throughout the house was

5

6   Society for the Preservation of New England Antiquities, J. David Bohl photographer.

167

The Nickels-Sortwell house (this page) was built in 1807 by Capt. William Nickels to command a view of the Wiscasset, Me., harbor in which his ships berthed. Like many of the houses of that day, its design was taken largely from a pattern book by Asher Benjamin, one of New England's leading architects. If such books were available today and if modern builders would follow them without injecting their own bad ideas, our landscape would be far more beautiful. On the opposite page is the Wheeler-Banks house in Temple, N.H. It was built in 1798. The doorways on front and side are identical. At some time, probably long ago, the sills of the windows in the first-floor front rooms were dropped about 6 inches while those in the kitchen were not. This is apparent in the picture below, right.

1

2

3

4

170

5

6

The Wheeler-Banks house (continued from the preceding page) has a Federal exterior but a typical Colonial plan and Colonial and Georgian interior treatment. 1 is the dining room and 2 the living room. 5 is an upstairs chamber; 6, the old kitchen (now a family room). 3 is the upstairs hall. The wainscot is made of horizontal boards as in the rest of the house; the balustrade is an unusual solid panel. 4 shows one of the old interior doors and hardware. Like doors in other early small houses, it is little more than an inch thick; on the front side the panels are chamfered and flush with the frame but flat and recessed on the back. 7 is the base of the chimney. In earliest days this was either a mass of stone or a retaining wall surrounding solid unexcavated soil. Arching the base was a later idea but not used too often.

7

The Rundlet-May house (this page) was built in 1812. It is another of Portsmouth's great Federal houses and has been changed little by the two families that occupied it. Compare the delicacy of the banisters with the Georgian banisters shown earlier. The house on the facing page was built in South Woodstock, Vt., in 1817. Not in the least ostentatious, it is just one of those charming brick houses of which the Federal era produced a good many. The wood-frame wing is fairly recent. The middle picture at top shows one of the simple but effective ways old builders decorated window headings. The three windows above the fine front doorway are suggestive of Palladio but note that the sash themselves are not arched. In the blind arch over the center window is a painting of a horse.

1

2

3

Facing page: Interiors of the South Woodstock house on page 173. 1 is the old kitchen, now the dining room; 2, the living room. Because of the thickness of old brick walls, the reveals inside the windows are very deep, 3. The Asa Stebbins house in Deerfield is at 4 and 5. The front was built in 1810; the rear wing in 1799. 6 is the Capt. Gamaliel Bradford house in Duxbury, Mass. Few other country homes had arched windows flanking the doorway.

4

5

6

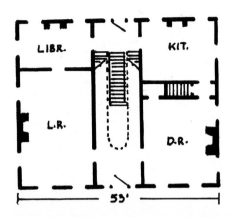

The Sweat house in Portland, Me., was built in 1800. The architect was Alexander Parris, another of the famed Boston designers. He created a house notable for delicate detail. This is apparent outside in the roof balustrade and the splendid portico — especially the balustrade on the roof of the portico. Note that the window heights on all three floors are different. The house is a typical four-room-and-center-hall plan. The stairway rises in the center of the hall to a landing and doubles back for five steps on both sides. The balustrade continues along the hall, ending in a curve at the front (dotted line on plan). Thus a well unites the two levels of the hall and helps to brighten the first-floor level.

The Greek Revival style was sweeping the country about the time that the whalers of New Bedford were starting to make their fortunes. Some magnificent houses were the result. This is the William R. Rodman house, built in 1835. In design and size, you might take it for a museum or bank.

GREEK REVIVAL

What happened in New Bedford happened in New London for the same reasons: whaling made the town boom and the town responded by building Greek Revival homes. Whale Oil Row, above and left, was built on speculation in the 1830s. The houses are not identical but not very different. All have two-story porticoes supported by giant Ionic columns. The houses fell into disrepair and their existence was in jeopardy until they were restored as office buildings some years back. Unfortunately, the restoration was not always good: one house is clad in asbestos shingles. The Russell house, right, was built in Middletown, Conn., in 1828 and is now part of Wesleyan University. It was designed by the stellar Greek Revival architects, Ithiel Town and Alexander Jackson Davis, and is far richer in texture than the New London homes. The columns are Corinthian. They were meant for a New Haven bank.

This gem was designed by Ithiel Town for Charles Daniels and built in Chester, Conn., in 1826. Later used as a warehouse, it was rescued by Thomas A. Norton, New York and Chester architect. The house has four rooms on the main floor. The double parlors, above, are right of the hall. Since the land falls off to the rear, dining room (far right) and kitchen are in the basement. Bedrooms are on the top floor. The monitor at the roof peak has a skylight that lights the main hall and stairs. An old back stair, right, spirals from the basement to the top floor without stopping at the main floor.

180

H. Durston Saylor.

The Stephen Salisbury II house was built in Worcester in 1836. It is a very unusual Greek Revival house with its wreath-encircled round windows in the frieze, Gothic hood molds over the windows, which are recessed about 6 inches, and its one-story Doric porch. Inside, a circular stair rises to a second-floor rotunda with Corinthian columns supporting a shallow coffered dome with a skylight. On the facing page are two Greek Revival houses with wings at both ends. That at the top was built in Old Mystic, Conn., in 1833; the Salem Copeland house in Worcester dates from 1847. The former is the larger but the less elaborate, with relatively simple Ionic columns. The Copeland house has Corinthian columns, bracketed window cornices and the unusual, eye-catching carved frame around the gable window.

Although from the street the Rotch-Jones-Duff house in New Bedford appears quite low, the cupola, right, from which Rotch watched the harbor for the comings and goings of his whaling ships is almost invisible. Even from the garden the cupola is hidden by the balustrade along the eaves and because of the home's really great height. It is one of New England's handsomest houses of any style and is very well landscaped to boot. Built in 1834, it is just now being restored and is sparsely furnished. The rooms are high-ceilinged but have few of the decorative features one might expect in a house of this size. The wide hallway (facing page) is divided by a huge door. This was to keep Rotch's business visitors from entering the family living area. From the spacious entry inside the front door, they stepped into Rotch's office, which later owners combined with the dining room.

The houses at the top of these two pages are more or less conventional examples of the Greek Revival style. At left is the Gurdon Trumbull house, built in Stonington, Conn., in 1840. At right is the Willard house, built one year earlier in Orford, N.H. The latter is the only Greek Revival house among the seven homes that grace Orford's Ridge Row (see Page 148). The cupola of the Trumbull house provides a sweeping view of the Stonington harbor.

The two houses below are vernacular versions of the Greek Revival style. At left is the Connor-Bovie house in Fairfield, Me. The pilasters are slotted, with the slot in a darker color than the face. The same pilaster treatment is to be seen on other Maine houses. The house at right is in Castleton, Vt., where unusual architecture prevails. The windows have arched pediments as does the door. The decorated tympanum of the roof pediment is deeply recessed.

There is more variety in Greek Revival architecture than many people believe — as these fine houses demonstrate. Below is an impressive smallish house in Belfast, Me. On the facing page is the Charles Chandler Griswold house, built in Old Lyme, Conn., in 1842.

Above it is the Marvin-Griffin house, also in Old Lyme. Before 1820, the materials for the latter were precut in Albany and shipped down the Hudson for assembly. (One of the building industry's first attempts at prefabrication.) Wings and porch were added later.

The cornices above the windows and porticoes of the Kennebunk, Me., house above are not Greek Revival characteristics but the very low roof, wide cornice and unadorned frieze are. The Robert Nott house, right, has fewer idiosyncrasies, but the gable windows are one. The deep, two-story bay was added. The house was built in Kennebunkport in 1853. On the facing page, at top, is the Clark house in Old Lyme, Conn. Some of its charm is attributable to the unorthodox porch columns, window treatment and spire on the cupola. It was built in the 1840s. Below it is the Farnsworth house (1850) in Rockland, Me. Its severity is relieved by the carriage house.

While no one can deny the great beauty of the big Corinthian-columned Southport, Conn., house on the facing page, one must admit that there is also beauty in simplicity. Witness the two houses here. The pilastered, yellow Lord house in Lyme, Conn., was built in 1812. The white house in Belfast, Me., is a much younger and even simpler type that you see often, but rarely in such well executed form. At the top, opposite, is the 1833, Milton, Mass., home of Capt. Robert Forbes, a merchant who may have brought back from overseas some of the exotic feeling he put into the house.

These two houses more or less represent the extremes in Victorian architecture: the simple, straight-forward, clapboarded farmhouse with minimum decoration and the brick city mansion with bays and juts, uneven roofline and towering chimneys. The former was built without aid of architect by Capt. James Bill in Lyme, Conn., in 1866. The latter is the B.W. Crowninshield house, constructed in Boston four years later. It was designed by Henry Hobson Richardson.

Richardson ranks among our greatest architects and most of his work was done from an office in Brookline, Mass. The Crowninshield house was one of his first commissions and one of the few things about it suggestive of his later and best work is the arches adorning the base of the biggest chimney. In short, the house is not in the Richardsonian Romanesque style that made him famous.

VICTORIAN

The 1847 house in Windsor, Vt., above has all the marvelous ornamental features generally expected of Victorian. The chimneys in each pair are separated and set at forty-five degree angles to the ridge.

The date posted on the Hurlburt-Dunham house (facing page) in Wethersfield, Conn., says 1804. At that time it was of Federal design. But much later it was torn apart and redone in the Victorian manner. An improvement? Who's to say? But it's a very comfortable looking house and a nice foil for the ancient Georgians all around it.

The cozy Hansel-and-Gretel sort of house on the facing page and at left is called the Gingerbread House. In Essex, Conn., it is assumed to have been built by H.L. Pratt before 1858 but no one knows whether it had its gingerbread at that date — and who cares? It is the house most visitors to Essex seem to remember even though the town is rich in fine Federals. Below is the large Mills-Stebbins house in Springfield. It was built in 1851. Of the Italian Villa style, it makes an irregular silhouette against the sky and is alive with interesting features including oriels and the marvelous door canopy, which does double-duty as a second-story balcony.

Andrew Jackson Downing, America's foremost proponent of the Victorian style, wrote: "A blind partiality for any one style in building is detrimental to the progress of improvement." Perhaps taking their cue from this, Victorian architects had few inhibitions. Their houses, as a result, are fun to look at and live in. The Brooks house (1889) in Chester, Conn., is an example.

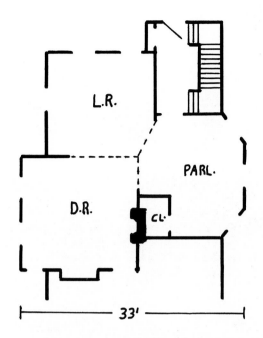

Its shape is beyond description. Its exterior walls are clad in clapboards, diagonal boards, fancy-shaped shingles. It has brackets, lacy ironwork on the tower, an oriel with stained glass, exposed scrolled rafters. Best of all is the interior, which because of many large windows is bright with light despite golden-oak woodwork. The living area (plan) is unique. Originally it had folding doors at the dotted lines so the three rooms could be closed off. These were long ago removed to make one big room; yet each area has privacy as well as individual character (the dining room ceiling, for instance, has plaster decoration). The beams carrying the ceiling are held up at the point where they meet by a steel rod extending to the roof ridge high above.

Across the top of both pages is the Godfrey-Kellogg house, built in Bangor in 1847. It is an extremely large Gothic cottage, spreading to the left of the camera (facing page). Though only a story-and-a-half high, the chimneys and scepter-like standards at the gable peaks give it strong verticality. At left is the Othniel C. Marsh house, built of unevenly colored brownstone in New Haven.

On the facing page, top, is the Stephen Thayer house (1838) in New Ipswich, N.H. Above is a Portland, Me., house of about the same date. Both are in the Gothic Revival style, though the latter is the better example because of its intricate bargeboards and sharply arched windows. The Thayer house's Gothic look stems only from the dark-painted arches above the windows and the Gothic-arch-shaped dormer roofs. At left is an octagonal house in Portland, Conn. Thomas Jefferson put up an octagonal house in Virginia in 1800, but it was not until Orson Squire Fowler wrote a book in 1850 extolling this design that it became popular.

No one is sure of the age of the Lyme, Conn., house above, but it began life as a Colonial in the late 1700s. Then, like many houses, it was turned into a Victorian, in part so the owners could sit on the veranda and enjoy the river view from it. All the other pictures here are of the Gothic-style William J. Rotch house in New Bedford. Built in 1846, it is one of the houses designed by Alexander Jackson Davis, the country's most prolific Gothic Revival architect. and illustrated in Downing's books on Victorian architecture. It is one of the outstanding Gothic Revival homes in the U.S. Among other things, note the variety of window shapes. The smooth flush-board walls form an ideal background for the bargeboards, doors, windows and porches.

206

The house at top, right, is a simple Italianate structure with typical bracketed eaves, low roof and cupola. It is the Stevens-Frisbie house in Cromwell, Conn. Below it is the enormous Lockwood-Mathews mansion in Norwalk, Conn. It is in the Second Empire style that was popular after the Civil War and is generally identifiable by a mansard roof and cast-iron roof crestings.

The Victorian styles were so varied and free of dogma that builders and home owners could and did have a field day designing their own vernacular versions. The house above is one of these. It is in the Johnsonville section of East Haddam, Conn. It's based on the Italianate style.

At right is an Italian Villa-style house in Lexington, Mass., almost within stone's throw of the green on which the first battle of the Revolution was fought. It was built in 1847 by a Colonel Chandler. Below is one of Newport's summer cottages. In size or beauty, it is not in the league with such cottages as Marble House or The Breakers but is the same sort of house that was built in the late 19th Century wherever the wealthy summered. It belongs to the Shingle style of architecture.

This long, low house in Thomaston, Me., is vernacular Victorian.
It is very simple and pleasant — not the kind of house that stops you
when you pass, but it stands out clearly from considerable distance.

The Wedding Cake house, below, in Kennebunk, Me., is purely romantic froth superimposed on a straight-forward structure. Imagine anyone today building such a place. The Augusta, Me., house at top, right, is a Georgian and Victorian composite. The house at bottom, right, is in the Second Empire style. By itself it would be handsome; with its attached carriage shed it is doubly so. It, too, is in Kennebunk.

1

2

214

Although the Worcester house at 1 is partially brick, it is of the Shingle style. It's the kind of house that you see repeatedly in New England cities. The wall in the lower half of the gable waves in and out. It must have given the carpenters fits to construct. At 2 is the Capt. Abijah Davis house in Oxford, Mass. It has elements of the Greek Revival style but is strongly Italianate. The ornate doorway at 3 is in a row house in Portland, Me. In its own way it is about as fine as any of the Georgian or Federal doorways shown. On Victorian houses, however, doorways did not bear the brunt of beautifying the facade because the houses had so many other eye-catching elements. 4 is the Converse house in Norwich, Conn. — an interesting Gothic Revival design especially because of its large polygonal porch.

3

4

1

3

1 — an attractive concoction in Belfast, Me. The glistening white ornamentation stands out against the gray flush-board siding. 2 — the 1870 Putnam-Balch house in Salem, Mass., holds its own well midst stiff Federal competition. 3 — the tower of the Frank Dingley house in Auburn, Me. Its protruding round windows are startling. 4 — The Joseph Low house in Bangor is effective but grim looking. 5 — the Gilbert Russell house in New Bedford is said to date from 1805. If true, this would make it a very early Victorian. It may have started life as something else.

2

4

5

Hillhouse Avenue in New Haven was conceived to be a street of Greek Revival homes, of which Town and Davis were the main architects. But Ithiel Town didn't keep a tight rein on a young protégé who preferred Italian Villas — and designed the one above. Left: The fact that the Victorian style followed and to some extent overlapped the Greek Revival style accounts for the many homes that fall into both categories, as this one in Brunswick, Me., does. On the facing page: Second Empire style in Kennebunk, Me. The house is a delight from its sweeping solid front-step railings to the fancy ironwork that crowns the mansard roof and tower.

On this page, top, an 1875 Italian Villa built by Henry Lord in Old Lyme, Conn. Originally it had a tower, but that went down in the 1938 hurricane. The present owner may restore it. At left is a Second Empire house in Suffield, Conn. Opposite, top, is a wonderfully gingerbreaded house in a section of Middletown, Conn., where gingerbread is plentiful. Below it is a brick Victorian in Hatfield, Mass. Its slate roof is decorated as lavishly as the facade.

Although the mansard roof is associated with Francois Mansart, a French architect who died in 1666, he did not invent it. But its attribution to him indicates it's a very old idea. Victorian architects picked it up and used it widely, especially in houses of Second Empire design. A modification of the hip roof, the mansard rises steeply from the eaves on the four sides of a house, then slopes gradually toward the peak. The lower slope may be straight, concave or convex. These two Victorians offer good examples of the roof. The house above was built in Hatfield, Mass., in 1865. At right is the Blake house in Bangor.

INDEX